# TEN OF DIAMONDS

## Tony Jones

**THE STORY OF RUSHDEN AND DIAMONDS FOOTBALL CLUB**

Ten of Diamonds
Tony Jones ©

All rights reserved. No part of this publication may be produced, stored in a retrieval system or transmitted in any form or by any means, electronic, mechanical, photocopying, recording or otherwise, without permissions in writing from A.C Publications.

ISBN: 0-9543708-0-5

First published in 2002
By A.C Publications, Manor Drive, Irthlingborough, Northamptonshire, NN9 5SL

Printed and bound by Woolnough Bookbinders, Church Street, Irthlingborough, Northamptonshire, NN9 5SE

*Max Griggs C.B.E.
Relaxing at Nene Park.*

# FOREWORD

Most football followers bear an allegiance to a particular team. Week in and week out, they diligently follow its fortunes from the terrace or nervously await James Alexander Gordon's dulcet tones as he reads the classified results on 'Sports Report'. I know of a Burnley supporter from Market Harborough, who has named his house 'Turf Moor', painted it claret and blue and offers prayers on his knees before a photograph of the 1960 First Division Championship winning side every night before he goes to bed. Not unreasonably, they consider themselves to be true fans. Yet this devotion pales into insignificance when compared with that rare breed who turn allegiance into commitment and, crucially, commitment into action.

While watching League football in the comfort and splendour of the Nene Park Stadium, supporters might reflect upon two thought-provoking observations from the not too distant past.

The Kettering and District Amateur League handbook from 1961-62 informs us that, "Irthlingborough Diamonds change for matches in a room at the 'Sow and Pigs' public house"

Five years later, after the side had won the Second Division of the United Counties League by a handsome margin, this report appeared in the local 'Football Telegraph', familiarly known as the "Pink 'Un". "The one dark cloud ever present over the Diamonds is the lack of a pitch they can call their own. The problems created by having to use a council-owned ground have been well aired this season. They will get bigger as the club tries to improve its status."

Many people have contributed to the rise and rise of the Diamonds over the years, but the seeds of success were sown by an enthusiastic visionary who nurtured and utilised that support, turning an improbable dream into reality. His association with the club, which began with its founding in 1947, has coincided with its progress from the Rushden and District Youth League to the Nationwide Third Division, from the Manton Road Recreation Field to the Millennium Stadium.

This is Tony Jones' personal account of that remarkable journey. No one is better qualified to tell the tale.

Ian Addis

# ACKNOWLEDGEMENTS

In writing this book, I have called upon various people for information, assistance and understanding.

Particularly, I would like to thank Rebecca Thomas who typed up every word from my reams of scribbled notes.

To Ken Ambridge, who supplied me with much information and background stories of Rushden Town Football Club.

To Paul Redding, our club photographer, for the use of many splendid pictures.

To Andrew Bubeer, our Club Commercial Manager, for his concise explanations of the intricacies of computerised technology, and his overall assistance.

To Andrew Langley, for presenting me with the book 'The Miracle of Castel di Sangro', which initially inspired me into writing this book.

To Ian Addis, an old football friend of many years who held my hand when it came to the final compilation, and for his statistical input throughout.

To Steve Spooner (our First Team Coach), for suggesting the title, "Ten of Diamonds".

To Tony Wheatley of Blue Green Design Consultants of Bedford, for providing the outer cover layout – free gratis.

To my wife Jean, for allowing me the countless hours of necessary solitude in putting pen to paper and also for her understanding and support over a very long time.

**Finally, I would like to dedicate this book to Max Griggs, without whom there would be no story to tell.**

# INTRODUCTION

I first got the idea of writing this book when I was sitting in the warm evening sun whilst in Spain in early June of this year (2002).

I was reading the Joe McGinniss book, "The Miracle of Castel di Sangro", which is a true story of how he, an American, fell in love with the game of football and went to live in Italy for a whole season.

The football club, Castel di Sangro, had risen through the pyramid system of Italian football, from an amateur club to the professional ranks in reaching Serie B (one division below the top premier league) - an incredible rise of eight divisions over a fifteen-year period.
He lived with, and was closely involved with, the players and officials of the club throughout the season. The story inspired me into thinking more and more about the Rushden and Diamonds Football Club, its origins, its people, past and present, its success and the stories behind the scenes.

The more I thought about it, the more convinced I became that a book should be written, commemorating Rushden and Diamonds' ten years in existence and their promotion to the Football League.

With the advantage of having been with the Irthlingborough Diamonds for the 45 years since conception, right through the 10 years of the hybrid Rushden and Diamonds, I considered that I had the most information and memories to undertake such an exercise. Although I had only limited knowledge of Rushden Town, I nevertheless was keenly aware of their background and activities over the years. The details that I didn't know, I simply researched. I have, therefore, put together the story of how and why the merger happened. Also I have endeavoured to give the reader an emotional and statistical feel of the original clubs and in particular of Rushden and Diamonds, who have just completed their first ever season as a Football League club.

# CONTENTS

|  |  | Page |
|---|---|---|
| Chapter 1 | 1992 – The Merger | 9 |
| Chapter 2 | The war is over – and football returns | 17 |
| Chapter 3 | Success and failure – it's a very thin line | 27 |
| Chapter 4 | I want Nene Park to be a fun place | 37 |
| Chapter 5 | Full Steam Ahead | 43 |
| Chapter 6 | The Joy of Promotion - Again | 51 |
| Chapter 7 | Saved by B.T | 59 |
| Chapter 8 | Conference Consolidation | 67 |
| Chapter 9 | Hospitality, Celebrities and the Emerald Isle | 75 |
| Chapter 10 | Expectations Abound | 91 |
| Chapter 11 | Second is nowhere and so unfair | 101 |
| Chapter 12 | Footballing Trips can be Fun (well most of the time) | 109 |
| Chapter 13 | Conference Champions At Last | 117 |
| Chapter 14 | The Football League – We've Arrived | 129 |
| Chapter 15 | Max Griggs, C.B.E | 151 |

# 1

# 1992 – THE MERGER

**THIS is the story of the football club that Max Griggs built. He was the captain – it was his dream. Many people made it work and contributed along the way, but he was the key man. It's an unlikely story in footballing terms and has been told many times over – often varying in actual content.**

But I was there at the beginning and therefore can relate exactly how it all came to be.

Two small local football clubs in East Northamptonshire were merged together, almost on a whim and football in that area changed forever. Nothing in life ever remains the same, let alone in football. Sometimes it may be through circumstances, incompetence, finance or even ambition, but sure enough, changes occur. Sometimes it just happens and other times they are made to happen.

Max Griggs wanted it to happen – and it happened.

Life itself is all about memories and I hope to take you on a journey which highlights some very memorable times.

The events that brought these two clubs together came about in the year 1992. It was to signal the end of both Rushden Town and Irthlingborough Diamonds Football Clubs and the birth of the Rushden and Diamonds Football Club. Even now, ten years on, there are people who recall the 'old days' with great affection and loyalty. Their original allegiances still lie with the particular club they supported and I still refer to the new club as the Diamonds, but fans on the terrace chant "Rushden Till I Die!"

Apart from relating the events of the last ten years, I also want to tell the background of both the original clubs – after all, a combined total history dating back one hundred and forty eight years is worthy of reflection. It is too long just to be dismissed as irrelevant – both clubs deserve better than that. Nevertheless, at the time when the merger was suggested, there was not too much aggravation from the Diamonds fans – then again, we didn't have many. In the main, the angry criticisms came more from Rushden Town fans and ex-players. They had a much longer history – and a bigger town.

There were many more people who valued Rushden Town's status. They regarded the Russians (their long-standing nickname) as a more senior club and technically speaking they were right – just. Equally they didn't like the idea of their town club cavorting with the enemy from the other side of the River Nene, only three miles away.

Why should they?

What they didn't realise or didn't want to accept was that Rushden Town, just like Irthlingborough Diamonds, were in real trouble.

The old stand of Hayden Road, which had seen countless wonderful days full to capacity, was now dangerous and falling apart. The Southern League had insisted that Rushden Town

# Ten of Diamonds

*Hoyden Road, Rushden*

either replace the old stand altogether or carry out major work on the existing one, which would have cost a very considerable sum of money – and on a ground which they did not own.

Considerable efforts were made by their chairman Neil Gant to acquire land just outside the town but at each turn he was thwarted for one reason or another in an attempt to give Rushden Town a new home.

Whilst all of this was going on in Rushden, I had reached a time in my life when decisions had to be made. The Irthlingborough Diamonds Football Club of which I was chairman had been in existence for 45 years; since 1947, when together with other youngsters, I had helped start the club. I felt the club had run its course.

It had been a very successful club but the passionate hard-working band of committee people were, like me, finding it hard going. Money was short, enthusiasm on the wane, and nobody was getting any younger.

Sunday morning car boot sales at the old Nene Park just allowed us to pay the bills. It was, for me, the lowest time at the club. I didn't want to give up on all that we had worked for and built over the years, but I was feeling decidedly frayed and tired of constant struggle. The golden years of the four United Counties League (UCL) championships and twice F.A Vase semi-finalists were in the past.

By January 1992, I had made a single-minded decision. I would try to find someone to take over the Irthlingborough Diamonds Football Club. Perhaps a new younger guy could inject the necessary drive and stimulus required. If I could find someone with a business background and a bit of money who might like the idea of having his own football club – then maybe, just maybe, the Irthlingborough Diamonds might be saved.

*The original Nene Park, Irthlingborough*

But who?

At this stage, I had not discussed my thoughts with my fellow committee members but I intended to do so once I had something concrete on the table.

Ideally, it would have been nice to find someone who had been a player at the Diamonds and who now had his own business. That way, the person would have a feel for the club. I listed the people who were possibilities – there were very few. It was soon reduced to two candidates. Both were in their own business but one had a good accountancy background – that was what it needed.

# 1992 – The Merger

*Peter Phipps*

Peter Phipps was my choice.

'Phippy' had twice been a player with the Diamonds – that was a plus. The only likely downside was that his business venture was beginning to take off and would require most of his time and efforts.

Nevertheless – I had to try.

I knew Peter very well, having previously persuaded him to come back to the Diamonds for a second spell as a player. Could I sell him the idea of returning a third time as chairman? That was the big one. I telephoned him for an appointment, not telling him what I wanted from him. I visited his office and he listened intently to my proposals but at the end of the allotted half hour, Peter said, "Tony – thanks, but no thanks".

One down, one to go.

Number two on my list was Barry Hancock, who was another Northampton lad who had played centre half for Diamonds several years earlier. Barry was in the packaging business but the one disconcerting aspect was that he had only recently become involved with the Cobblers at Sixfields. This was a major stumbling block, but I had to give it a try.

I telephoned Barry and on this occasion explained my thoughts over the phone. He was mildly interested and said that he would think about it. I was not optimistic. A few days later, he phoned me back and declined my offer of the keys to Nene Park.

Now I was really struggling.

Then I thought, 'Why does it have to be an ex-player?' I really did think long and hard about it. Who did I know who was a businessman, a football lover and who might just want a club of his own?

Then it hit me – why not give Max Griggs a call?

I had met Max recently when our company Abbey Vogue Footwear had sold two small factory units, together with the staff to the Griggs Group. It was the time when the Dr Martens empire was expanding rapidly and they had required much needed extra stitching capacity. The two separate deals had been concluded very amicably and quickly. Afterwards, we had chatted about Max and his love for football and also about his unsavoury demise as a director of Northampton Town. As a board member, he had been hounded out of County Ground (where they played before Sixfields was built) by a section of fans and a local sports reporter.

He felt badly wounded but still loved the game. That was the catalyst for my third attempt to find a new owner for the Diamonds. I discussed my thoughts about approaching Max with my two business partners, Robert Langley and Chris Smith. They had been at the meetings when we had met Max about the factories. We agreed it was worth a shot.

One must bear in mind that although neither of them were directly involved with the Diamonds at that particular time, Robert had been club treasurer for many years previously, whilst Chris had been a player twice and the manager twice.

I telephoned Max suggesting a meeting.

He said, "I suppose you are looking for sponsorship?" "No", I replied, "but I have an idea for your company that might well be of interest to you", I added.

So we met.

We had our meeting at the Cobbs Lane offices of the Griggs Group in Wollaston, where a row of old stone cottages had been nicely converted into offices and a boardroom. Max's

# Ten of Diamonds

grandfather had once lived in one of the cottages, so obviously there was a great sentimental attachment. However could I convince him of my proposal?

For this first meeting, Robert came along with me and Max's son Stephen was also present. I had with me a typed business plan which set out my suggestions for the Griggs Group to take over the football club, lock stock and barrel, including the additional 3.5 acres which the club had bought separately and had not developed.

My idea was that the company would immediately have a Sports & Social club base for its 2,000 plus employees, land to develop as they saw fit and last but not least a football club – the Irthlingborough Diamonds. There was a lot more detail but that was the nub of it.

Max said, "I'll think about it"

I had heard that before!

So ended my third attempt on finding a new boss for the Diamonds – a maybe.

Two weeks went by with not a word from Max, so I telephoned again, but was obviously anxious not to appear too pushy. He said that he still wanted to discuss it with the other members of his board, so again I just had to wait.

Then a letter arrived. Could this be the answer to my prayers?

No! It was a confirmation that he was still considering my proposal. But it wasn't an outright rejection. Then came the phone call that was to change the direction of my life and in time, thousands of others. Not that I knew that then.

Max suggested that he and two other directors – son Stephen and Mark Darnell should come over to our factory in Burton Latimer. A quick tour of our Abbey Vogue factory immediately set the tongues wagging amongst the workforce. We learned afterwards that our workers were convinced that Griggs Group was about to buy out Abbey Vogue and add them to their ever-growing list of purchases. If only!

Actually, it was never even discussed as our type of shoe machinery and layout was not conducive to the Dr Martens range. More the pity! It was football that was on the agenda that famous day – not shoes.

Chris Smith joined the party and the six of us had lunch at the 'Old Victoria' pub in Burton Latimer. All very pleasant, but it was time for the real business – I crossed my fingers – it was now or never.

Yes, they were interested.

Max outlined a few thoughts for possible future improvement but then asked what sort of initial financial input was necessary to get things moving. I couldn't believe what I was hearing. It really did seem that something exciting was going to happen, but it had not been made clear just how.

Max then said that we could form a new board of directors – the six people present at the lunch. That was Max, Stephen, Mark from the Griggs company, together with Robert, Chris and myself from the Diamonds (or Abbey Vogue for that matter). He then asked what amount of starting capital was required to get things moving. Robert, ever quick when it came to discussing money, said, "£20,000 should get us started"

"OK", replied Max.

I gulped – an injection of £20,000 would have kept the old Irthlingborough Diamonds going for years! Although it had always been my intention to bow out gracefully and let a new chairman take over, with a complete new slate, Max insisted that he wanted me around, "to show me the ropes", as he put it.

Handshakes all the way round – the Irthlingborough Diamonds were now safe. A few weeks earlier I had persuaded John Brown, who was one of our key employees at Abbey Vogue and a real football nut, to take over temporarily as manager of the Diamonds. He was very reluctant but I convinced him that it wouldn't be for long – probably for the remainder of the season, from January to the end of April. I couldn't tell him what was in the pipeline but had said it could be something that would turn the club around.

# 1992 – The Merger

After the lunch at the 'Old Victoria', I returned to our offices in dreamland. I think all three of us were still reeling. I went to see John Brown immediately.

"John, I've got some great news for us – you're out of a job!" I blurted out. "It will be a few days before I can reveal all the details as there will be a press announcement shortly", I added.

A lovely man, John. He was similarly delighted that the Diamonds would be saved, and it was John who designed our new club crest from the originals of both clubs. However, I now had another hurdle to clear. Whilst I had kept my footballing committee informed that discussions were taking place regarding the club's future, I had not been able to reveal who, what and where.

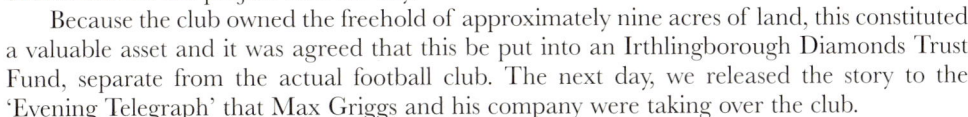

*John Brown*

I called an emergency meeting and laid out the plans, both financial and organisational. I explained that whilst the new Board of Directors would handle financial matters and overall policy, the committee would still be kept intact to deal with normal routine activities. My enthusiasm for the project won the day.

Because the club owned the freehold of approximately nine acres of land, this constituted a valuable asset and it was agreed that this be put into an Irthlingborough Diamonds Trust Fund, separate from the actual football club. The next day, we released the story to the 'Evening Telegraph' that Max Griggs and his company were taking over the club.

In the meantime, the club would play out its remaining fixtures under John Brown. It was undoubtedly the weakest squad that the Diamonds had ever had since joining the UCL and the club finished the season in 17th place out of 22. But who cared?!

A couple of days later, Max and two of his Griggs Group directors went to Nene Park just to see what their chairman had let himself in for. He was, by this time, dead keen and raring to go. He outlined his thoughts for a new big stand on the opposite side to the existing stand. He wanted the clubhouse painting and smartening up. Then Max made the first of his many famous statements.

"I think we could reach the Conference in five years"

"Dream on, Max", I thought, but dare not say. We were only a UCL club which would mean getting three promotions to reach the Conference – and in five years?!

By this time, Max was in regular contact with me, throwing up new ideas by the day. However there was no way that I could ever envisage his next proposal. It hit me like bombshell!

"I've been thinking about the league we play in. Rushden Town are also in a mess with their facilities and have been trying to get a new ground. Why don't we try and merge with them? We can play one league higher to start with", said Max.

Just like that! If only it could be that simple.

"Are you serious?" I replied, not liking the idea one little bit. Apart from getting Rushden Town to agree to a merger, I had to convince the Diamonds committee and my two business colleagues. Initially I recall Robert Langley was not over enamoured but Chris Smith was OK about it, having been a player at both clubs.

My committee at the Diamonds must have been wondering as to whatever was coming next. They were nonplussed by the speed of events. So was I. They didn't like the idea at all, but reluctantly agreed to play along and the thought of joining two committees together was likely to prove difficult.

The next problem lay with the Football Association in accepting the merger, and then the Southern League management into agreeing that a new merged club could take over Rushden Town's position in the Midland Division.

# Ten of Diamonds

Then we would have to get the ground up to a new standard and also increase the seating capacity. Next we must appoint a manager and find players of the necessary quality to compete at the higher level. Oh – and what about a set of fans!

Well one thing was for certain, the new boss was certainly laying down some new ground rules in a hurry. "Max, I'll see what I can do" I assured him.

I made contact with Neil Gant and he immediately saw the advantages from his point of view. If Irthlingborough Diamonds had succeeded in getting the Griggs Group behind them, then it would make more sense to join up with them, rather than continuing to try and find a new ground for Rushden Town and run the risk of the Diamonds overtaking them in status by virtue of the financial backing.

The Rushden Town committee were also informed of the distinct possibility of throwing their lot in with the enemy and were similarly sceptical but prepared to consider. A meeting was called in the clubhouse at Nene Park of both sets of committees. Those representing both clubs stood in two groups facing each other whilst it was explained how such a merger could take place and just how they as people could fit into the new set-up.

Whilst they were not exactly glaring at each other with suspicion, the feeling of resentment was quite evident. I remember well carefully explaining Max's proposals for the new merger, pointing out the obvious advantages and ignoring the downsides. After all, quite a few other non-league clubs have merged their resources but how successful I wasn't at all certain.

Tooting and Mitcham had been together a long time – Windsor and Eton, and Erith and Belvedere had also joined forces. I think most of these mergers had been born out of desperation rather than a charter for eventual success. I suppose in recent years, Dagenham and Redbridge were the most senior club to blossom in this manner, and they had actually engulfed yet another club along the way.

Interestingly, all the clubs mentioned, and there are a couple of others, have all been from the London conurbation.

I wonder why?

Also, there have not been any two Football League clubs to take the plunge, although over the years there has been much talk, but with larger fan bases it would have been very difficult. However it had been done at a full professional level in Italy where Sampdoria was the result of such a marriage over fifty years ago. Two clubs, Sampierdaronese and Andrea Doria who were situated in an area well recognised for its nouveaux-riche residents agreed to pool their resources but that was hardly Rushden and Irthlingborough!

In truth, I still had great reservations but I pushed ahead nonetheless. The problem of the two committees was overcome without too much rancour. There would obviously be casualties with people doing identical jobs at both clubs. There were two club secretaries from which to choose one, but ironically, neither had the job and Dave Joyce was confirmed as the secretary, and still is today.

So what about a name for the club?

Somehow we had to conjure up a name that would be acceptable to all concerned. Bearing in mind that the new club was to play in Irthlingborough at the existing Nene Park, one could argue that the name of the town of Irthlingborough should be included in the first name.

*David Joyce*

# 1992 – The Merger

However I was very anxious that the name of the Diamonds be kept – it was an excellent name and so synonymous with the original club. To keep the name, I felt it equally important therefore to have the name, Rushden, first. Something had to give, so Irthlingborough had to go. We all agreed, and so Rushden & Diamonds was about to be unveiled.

We were managing to create news in our local press regularly but whilst we were banging the drum loud and clear, the two sets of fans were very hesitant. It is interesting that neither club had many supporters at their home matches and virtually none for away games – but suddenly there was a lot of anger and criticism from all directions.

Many had not even been to any games, but now parochialism was starting to run deep. Some Rushden Town supporters said they would never set foot at a stadium in Irthlingborough and to this day, they never have done. Dave Joyce's main priority was to get the Football Association's approval for the merger. The fact that he was a member of the Northamptonshire FA Council and could convince his colleagues there was certainly a good starting point.

Anyway, we got the nod from the FA headquarters at Lancaster Gate and then our request for the new club to take Rushden Town's place in the Southern League was also agreed. Things were moving in the right direction. Neil Gant, as Rushden Town's chairman, was added to the board of directors so the six became seven.

Throughout all of these events occurring at commendable pace, I couldn't help wondering what my good friend and colleague David Knighton would have said about it all.

*Roger Ashby*

David, who had been a true Diamond as a youth team player, a committee member at 17 years of age and my Vice Chairman for many years, had died at the dreadfully young age of 48 in 1988.

I know that he would have fought me hard and passionately as he did on many occasions. He wouldn't have liked it one little bit, but I know he would have eventually come to accept it – and what a tremendous asset he would have been in today's club.

As regards the facilities at the ground, we had to get moving fast. In the existing stand, which was part seating and part standing, we added extra seating to make it all seater – how very grand "all seater" sounded!

I even recall that on a cleaning up day when all hands on deck were busy tidying up the stand, that Max turned up with a large sweeping brush and joined in!

Now it was time to turn our attention to the playing side – and probably more importantly – to appointing a manager.

It was also agreed that in the remaining two months of the '91-92 season, that Rushden Town would let the Irthlingborough Diamonds have a couple of players to bolster their struggling side and the Diamonds only one player who might figure in the new set up was Peter Clarke, who then switched to Rushden for a few games. All very entente cordial.

The Russians had a good nucleus of players, all of whom had contracts which expired at the end of that season. All agreed to join the new Rushden & Diamonds club for the following season. As for the manager, I recall that we did discuss two or three possible candidates but agreed that Roger Ashby should be our man.

Roger had a very good local pedigree, both as a player then a manager. He had played at Kettering Town as a right back under many managers and became the longest serving player in the club's history with 662 number of appearances.

15

# Ten of Diamonds

I had persuaded Roger to join us at the Diamonds as player/manager and he figured it was the right move coming at the right time – and so it proved. Roger joined the Diamonds in 1980 after Tony Sabey had told me of his intention to resign. Tony had enjoyed a very successful stint at Nene Park but wanted to concentrate on his business, although he did eventually emerge again at Hayden Road in a general managerial role.

Anyway, Roger similarly was very successful at Nene Park, adding two more UCL titles to the club's honours board, won four separate knock-out trophies in one season and had two FA Vase semi-final appearances.

He resigned in December 1985 on a matter of principle, went to Wolverton Town and then onto Rushden Town where he resurrected the club which had been in dire straits prior to him joining.

So Roger was the man to lead us into our first ever season as Rushden & Diamonds. In addition to his existing Rushden Town players, he added Ollie Kearns, an experienced league player who was now coming to the end of his career. John Flower, a six foot three giant of a centre half who had been with Aldershot in their dying days of Football League status, was also signed and the diminutive Adie Mann, who had been the youngest ever player for Northampton Town in the Football League at 16 years of age.

Adie was an exciting player who was to play an important role over the next three years at Nene Park. Mark Bushell, another who had been a youngster at the Cobblers, and goalkeeper Kevin Shoemake from Redbridge Forest (soon to become Dagenham and Redbridge) completed the summer signings. Glenville Donegal, another ex-Cobbler was to join after only two games and became the club's leading scorer that season.

So we were now all set on the pitch as well.

The new adventure was about to begin. Where it would take us, no one knew – certainly nobody could have ever envisaged what was to follow.

# 2
# THE WAR IS OVER – AND FOOTBALL RETURNS

**WHEN you are just kids, you don't understand what a world war of such horror and magnitude really means.**

The fact that millions upon millions of people lost their lives in a six-year period is incomprehensible to a lad who was only thirteen years of age when it ended.

I well remember the air raid sirens, warning of German aircraft approaching and a crippled British plane crash-landing in the garden fields next to my aunt's house opposite Pine Lodge in Wellingborough Road, Irthlingborough.

Although very young, I followed the latter stages of the war – we were winning by then – and I was allowed to have a large map on the wall of our council house living room. I plotted the progress of the various armies by sticking coloured pins in the map – much like in Brian Talbot's office, but his map only shows the destinations of the forthcoming oppositions!

Once the war was over, things started to get back to normal – but only slowly. Food rationing was still in place and coupons for clothes were required. In fact, when us young lads got together to discuss forming a team, we were unable to buy proper football shirts – they just were not available, and in any case, where could we get all those dreaded clothing coupons that had to be submitted to the shops?

Once it was established that we were going to be called The Diamonds, there was a simple answer. We would all get a white shirt each and our mothers would sew a red diamond onto the shirt. The fact that the cut diamond pieces of material might differ in size and that the white shirts were probably all different types of material simply did not matter. We were up and running.

So the Irthlingborough Diamonds – the nearest name to Dynamos (of Moscow fame) which we could think of, came into being.

A year or so later, I recall my mother cadging coupons from friends so that we could buy our first set of proper shirts. They were all red with lace-up fronts.

Our next main requirements were goalposts. In our friendly games, we had been using wooden stakes, similar to the old fashioned clothes lines, with a rope strung across as a crossbar. Primitive, yes, but beggars can't be choosers and we had no money for anything better.

Because we had St Peter's Church connections, having held our first formative meeting in the belfry, we decided to try and exploit the connection. Even at that young age we were streetwise enough to use any contact we might have – and in any case, we had no other alternatives.

The Reverend Reginald Sleight was that contact and we just asked him if he would be prepared to pay for our new proper wooden goalposts.

He said he would.

# Ten of Diamonds

So down to Thompson Brothers in Irthlingborough I went with a team-mate – I can't remember who. Yes, he would make them but there was a problem – it was immediately after the war and they could not get pieces of wood a full and complete 24 feet in length.

"But we can join three pieces of 8 feet together", said Mr Thompson. "OK", I said.

The crossbar was bolted together and quickly sagged in the middle. Who cared – it was better than the rope.

So, we commenced our 1947 first seasons in the Rushden and District Youth (under 18's) League with a sagging crossbar. But that's not the end of the story.

Several weeks passed and we assumed the invoice must have been paid by the Reverend Sleight. Anyway, nothing more was thought about payment until one fine day we received a reminder of the outstanding account. I can't remember how much it was for but in any case, we had no money.

In the meantime, the Reverend Sleight had moved on – I don't mean he had died, but he had taken up a new post, goodness knows where.

Well, I managed to find out his address from our new rector and so I wrote a nice polite letter enclosing the Thompson Brothers invoice and never heard another word. I can only assume that the Reverend Sleight paid up!

We played in a field, which today is the Huxlow School at the top of Finedon Road. The pitch was on a slope and we initially had to chop down hundreds of small wild scrubby bushes to clear a big enough area to set out a pitch. We changed in dressing rooms in Board Street, which is in the middle of Irthlingborough and it was a wooden upstairs building – more like a shack to which we had climb the very rickety outside stairs. It was at the back of some shops at the bottom end of Board Street and a very long way from the pitch.

We would then walk or maybe jog along College Street, up Scarborough Street, across the Recreation ground, through a gap in the hedge and up into the field where out pitch was still another 200 yards or so at the top end.

At the end of the match, all muddy and probably downhearted, we would do the journey in reverse – I would think it would be about a mile – but at least the return leg was all downhill.

My father would be at the Board Street dressing room where a tin bath with hot water awaited. The bath was only the size for one person sitting down or maybe three standing up, which was the way that we sponged down our muddy knees.

I can't be certain but I think the opposition used to go back home – Finedon, Rushden, Raunds or Wellingborough – to have a bath at their own homes. I know I did whenever we played away. although it was all so very primitive, we never thought twice about it. that's the way it was.

Father was an expert at blowing up footballs. None of today's simplicity. The footballs in those days were like suet puddings – very heavy and lacing them was an art in itself. No good kicking with the instep and side foot. The ball had to be toe-ended with the trajectory of a missile. For those who chose to head the ball, the impact was horrendous – or certainly appeared to be. Head tucked into shoulders, eyes firmly closed.

In the three years up to 1950 we continued in the same under 18's local league. We obviously didn't have anyone coaching us and we weren't very good – just enthusiastic.

Our one big hate was playing away to Wellingborough United Minors. As the name may indicate, they were attached to a proper men's team and this, the Under 18's, was their third team.

Not only were they much too good for us, but they also played on the dreaded Bassetts Close. There were two pitches side by side and they were on the most incredible slope imaginable. It could have doubled for a ski slope. If you don't believe me, then go along and see for yourself. Bassetts Close is still there today!

I can recall all of the lads who played together in those early days quite vividly. Little did

# The War Is Over – And Football Returns

any of them realise that they would be the forerunners of the Diamonds of today.

Unfortunately some are no longer with us but there are certainly a few who are season ticket holders and sit in the North Stand every match.

So who were they?

Well, let's start with the last line of defence.

I don't know why they call it that because I was the goalie and not the most reliable. I was called Jonah, which might explain why so much went wrong. Now it is true to say that I did lose my place once to a deputy – a lad called Clonny Marlow but because I was on the selection committee, I was soon reinstated!

Now it seems to me that nearly all the kids had nicknames, unlike today when names like Unders, Sutch, Butts and Burge are all abbreviations. One of the more splendid names was Bolang Billett. His real name was Robert but this was 1946 for heaven's sake! Bolang was our right back and skipper. He was as tough as old boots with a kick like a 6-inch mortar. As a senior player he later turned out for Higham Town and then emigrated to Perth, Australia, although I had lunch with him in Strikers about three years ago.

The original left back was George Slawson. He was one of the brighter boys which probably accounted for his ability to either misjump or slip over whenever the ball was travelling at great speed towards his head. His eventual replacement was a lad with another cracking nickname – Weaser. Keith Pratt was his lesser known name and he, like all good left backs, never kicked with his right foot – a bit like Unders today. Weaser still lives in Irthlingborough to this day.

There was no such thing as centre backs, whether it be two or even three – just one simple centre half. Ours was called Dummy – he never knew that it was his nickname because the poor lad was a deaf mute. His name was Geoff Coles, a smashing, lovely lad. He and I had a communication problem and often stared long and hard at each other when yet another soft goal was conceded. He married, left the area and I've never heard of him since – but I still remember him.

Today's midfielders were yesterday's wing-halves. Remember in those days there were always five forwards!

At wing half was Howard Freeman, known then and also to this very day at 'Fiddle'. How he came by such a questionable name I really don't know. He certainly didn't play one but maybe he was occasionally on it. What I do know was the he could play a bit and was certainly one of my best mates. Now the other wing half was a lad called Vic Kirk, and thereby lies a tale. He joined the Diamonds at the ripe old age of 17 and a half, and nobody dare give him a nickname because Vic had not only "done it" but was already a father. He certainly was our Godfather in an era of unmentionables.

Only some 35 years later did I discover that he was the father of our very own referee guru and betting afficionado, Bob Kirk – so there! I learned from Bob that his dad died in Yorkshire some five years ago.

Another of today's North Stand pundits was our centre forward. No strikers in those days, the word hadn't even been invented. Leon Horner was our front man, better known as 'Tubby'. Not because he was rotund, he fact he was built like the proverbial. His right footed toe pokers were legendary and so viscous that they would have caused devastation in a crowd behind the goal. They never did because there was only ever my dad and another bloke with his dog who stood at the opposite end. All the action was at t'other end!

Inside forwards usually had an intellectual air about them. Not for them, the rough and tumble of a muddy shirt.

They were the Grammar School boys and the dribblers of the team. Today we call them playmakers. Little Les Tyler who I recently saw at Nene Park, was partnered by the skinny languid Peter De Banke. They made us tick, or so they said. They were skilful and for some reason, neither had nicknames that I can recall.

# Ten of Diamonds

*1948/9 Irthlingborough Diamonds Under 18's
l-r back: F. Britchford, J. Simmons, K. Pratt, K. Lawrence, T. Jones, J. Parnell, P. Debanke, E. Hudson.
Front: H. Sherwood, L. Tyler, R. Billett, C. Davis, E. Long.*

Both later had lengthy careers with Rushden Town in the sixties. Les lives somewhere in Staffordshire, I think, while Peter lives on at Nene Park with you lads on his terrace.

We had three right wingers, or to be more precise, outside rights. I've no idea why we had three – but we did.

John Wills, John Simmons and Maurice Rawlins – all three were Irthlingborough boys and all were quick. John Wills no doubt tells all around him that he was as swift as Paul Hall. No John, you were not!

"Jenks" Simmons was a flyer and a strong one at that. A county schoolboy 400 yards champion, John and I were 'Best Man' at each other's weddings. Not a lot of people know that! Unfortunately John died a year or so ago.

The third of our right wing brigade was 'Moggy' Rawlins. Who on earth dreamt that name up I'll never know. A cat is quick and darting, and our 'Moggy' was certainly that, so perhaps that's the answer. Maurice still lives in Irthlingborough today.

Three others who played occasionally for the Diamonds in those early days were Brian Lewis, John Mayes and Peter Mitchell. Brian was one of the very early pioneers of the club and later became a senior policeman. John Mayes went to Kimbolton School and could only turn out when his school was not playing on a Saturday. He was a lovely lad, a cut above us local roughnecks, and later became a headmaster – perfect typecasting.

Now Peter Mitchell, that's another story to tell.

He played outside left, never tackled, never chased back, never headed the ball, but had the sweetest left foot imaginable. He also went to a private school and was therefore never a regular. He was also very well known in the shoe trade and eventually left quite rapidly to live in Spain! A charming chap.

# The War Is Over – And Football Returns

So much for the players – what about the backroom boys?

My father was head cook and bottle washer and was also chairman. Anything that needed doing, father did it – but more about him later.

Eric 'Soapy' Hudson was the trainer. There were no fancy names like physio. Eric was the good old fashioned bucket, sponge and cold water man. However the crème de la crème of our administration was none other than Frank Britchford.

Frank Britchford was the local milkman but always aspired to greater things in life. He was our club secretary – numero uno. Us kids called him 'lardie head', because of his heavily Brylcreamed hair, all black and slicked back – but not to his face!

He had this incredible ability to conjure up totally unheard of gobbledy-gook words whilst making Annual Dinner speeches. He also loved to sing at any opportunity – 'Underneath the Arches' – with his eyes closed tight – not the prettiest of sights! But Frank was a real character. How times have changed.

I suppose in years to come, people will talk about the players and officials of today (they have already started about one!) and relate stories of the old days. That's how it is in every generation.

By the time I was fast reaching the age when I would be too old to continue playing in he Youth Team, the side was slowly getting better. Could there be a connection?

In the season of 1950-51, we made the big time. Well, to be more exact, we won the Under 18 League for the first time! And the next season – and the season after that – and the next. In total we were champions of the Rushden and District Youth League five times in six years.

I had to make a personal decision – did I carry on playing as a moderate goalkeeper in which case I would have to try and get a game – maybe with Irthlingborough Town. Or did I want to concentrate on taking the Irthlingborough Diamonds forward? Although Frank Britchford was secretary at the time, I soon took over the reins and started nicking better players from other local Under 18 teams – hence our success.

We also won the NFA Under 18's Youth Cup, beating Northampton Town Youth 4-3 in the final with David Knighton who was to become an important cog in the Irthlingborough Diamonds story later on, scoring two of the goals.

In 1956 we decided it was time to move on.

We applied and were elected to the Rushden & District Men's League division 2 – this really was progress!

\*        \*        \*        \*        \*        \*        \*

Whilst all this activity had been happening in Irthlingborough, the football club three miles up the A6, namely Rushden Town, were back in their Senior Club environment. Rushden Town Football Club were so much higher in status and quality that they could have been a million miles away.

Who could ever have predicted that one day the boys of Irthlingborough and the men of Rushden would be united as one?

But whereas the Irthlingborough Diamonds only came into existence after World War 2, the Russians, as Rushden Town were known, had been a football club even before the First World War – 1889 to be precise.

The very first records which I could trace of Rushden Town Football Club was in an edition of the Evening Telegraph on Monday October 4th 1897.

The structure of the actual leagues is most confusing. For example, there was a league table for the Midland League and it showed Rushden Town in 3rd place behind Ilkeston and Chesterfield. Wellingborough Town were in the same league, as were Barnsley and Doncaster Rovers.

# Ten of Diamonds

I can only assume that the teams travelled by train as it was certainly before the advent of cars or coaches capable of undertaking such journeys.

One amusing story was contained in the newspaper regarding Finedon Revellers and Rushden Town Reserves, who apparently were playing in the Northants League, Division 1.

The game was advertised at 2.00pm but one team (not stating which) didn't arrive until 2.30pm. Rushden Town were due to play Wellingborough Town on the same pitch immediately after the other game finished. However having decided that it would not be possible to play two full 90-minute consecutive games, the Rushden Town reserves game finished at 3.30pm (ie, one hour playing time) and when the referee called time, Finedon were winning by 3-2.

Well that's one way of getting a result!

## RUSHDEN TOWN F.C. - 1948-49.

H. Penniss. R. Bland, V. Maddams, R. Martin, G. Andrews, K. Maddocks R. Hawtin,
(Treas.)  B. Inwood, (Trainer)
D. Mantle, S. Frost, G. Sail, L. Pipes, W. Burgess, W. Rochester, S. Toms.

Cyril Freeman became secretary of Rushden Town in 1919 after World War One ended. They struggled in the lower order regions until the 1924-25 season when they finished runners up. It was in 1926-27 that both the first team and their reserves were champions of their respective United Counties Leagues.

In the 1930's, Rushden Town were almost unbeatable. Their domination of the Northants League saw them champions six times in nine seasons – an amazing period of success.

Immediately after the Second World War ended, the Russians joined the United Counties League and although they won the League Knock-Out Cup in 1947 beating Wisbech Town 4-1, their pre-war league triumphs were not repeated.

# The War Is Over – And Football Returns

However the Russians did have a very promising pacy young left winger in Gordon Inwood. He was the son of Bert Inwood, who was a full back in the pre-war successful Rushden Town side. West Bromwich Albion signed son Gordon and he played at the Hawthorns for several years. With the money paid to the Russians (amount undisclosed, even in those days), the club put concrete terracing around the ground.

Reggie Bland, who had been a pre-war favourite player, was soon to become manager and players who became synonymous with the Russians of that time were Bob Clarke (Northants County cricketer), Geoff 'Sugar' Andrews, Stan Toms father of Mick, who starred for Irthlingborough Diamonds), Hoddy Childs, Len Pipes, Dennis Maddams, Ron Peacock (father of another Diamonds player, Bob) and Doug Mantle.

They were also producing young players good enough to step up to Football League status, and two who went to Nottingham Forest were both Rushden born lads – Dave Ballard and Fred Patenall. Interestingly, both these players starred with the Irthlingborough Diamonds in their Under 18 side prior to joining Rushden Town. During this time, I had a day off work and took the young Dave Ballard to Aston Villa for a trial where he played against Port Vale Reserves. Thirty years later I bumped into him quite by chance and he was then a Detective Sergeant in the West Midlands CID.

In the 1950-51 season, Rushden Town finished 4th in the United Counties League with Corby Town as champions. They were getting back to normal as a top senior side in the county.

The years of 1957, 1958 and 1959 in the Central Alliance League did not prove to be particularly fruitful for the Russians.

The new league which they had joined proved a little more difficult than anticipated. Peter de Banke was a regular at left half in their conventional 2-3-5 formation (was there ever any other? Not at that time!), a position he continued to play at Hayden Road for ten years.

The fact that Rushden Town finished the 1959-60 season only 8th in a league containing seventeen clubs (Bourne Town were champions) prompted them to consider switching back to earlier well-known pastures such as the United Counties League (UCL). However there was another overriding factor in this decision – the club was in financial trouble. They disclosed to the local press that they had a £700 overdraft! I am not sure what that really means in today's monetary terms but obviously it was serious enough for club secretary Ken Ambridge to lead the campaign for a change in direction.

It is interesting to note that in the Evening Telegraph, Ken stated that he had served on the committee for ten years and indicated that he wished to retire shortly. That was in 1960 and Ken eventually closed the door on his Rushden Town involvement in 1988 – another 28 years! Football gets you that way.

Also at that time, Rushden Town had a president, Bob Paragreen, who also acted as unpaid groundsman. He was a retired transport haulier who had a business called Paragreen & Mitchell, whose warehouse, stores and offices were on the site where today 'Exhibition and Interior" resides – opposite the Nene Park roundabout next to Central Garage. The other partner of his business had a son, Peter Mitchell, who was in the very first 1947 Irthlingborough Diamonds Youth Team.

Add to that the owner of Central Garage is Jeff Redding, who was to become for a short time also manager at Rushden Town some 30 years later. His three sons, Paul, Andy and Neil all played for Irthlingborough Diamonds or Rushden Town – or both. Now that really does mean keeping it in the family! But I digress.

Three miles away over the River Nene, Irthlingborough Diamonds were quietly on the march.

In 1957-58, they won the Rushden & District Division 2 again by a street. Although there were no requirements for automatic promotion or relegation within the league, I thought that we must move up into Division 1. I knew we had a side that was good enough, and so it

# Ten of Diamonds

proved that in the 1958-59, our first season, we were acclaimed champions.

The 1959-60 season came and went with the Diamonds finishing runners up and therefore at the end of that season it was decision time again. The Kettering and District Amateur League (KAL) was generally considered a tougher and better league than the Rushden and District, so we decided to give it a go.

1960-61 was the Diamonds first crack at the KAL but nonetheless finishing fourth in our initial attempt was OK. However 1961-62, we fell off the pace somewhat and a mini-slump saw us in 6th position.

The Russians, now back in the United Counties League, which was about two leagues higher in status than the Diamonds, ended up in 7th place. The following season of 1962-63 saw the Russians, managed by Terry Murray, on an upward trend finishing as runners up to their other neighbours, Wellingborough Town, who at that time had a fine semi-professional side which contained Mel Lloyd and Dennis Jones, both of whom became managers at Irthlingborough Diamonds.

Interestingly, there were only 14 sides in the UCL at that time, but this was to change dramatically in the next four years with a second division and a reserve league added. Confirmation that Rushden Town were now getting their act together saw them as champions of the United Counties League the following year.

Player/Manager was Charlie Marlow, a centre forward of considerable ability who had been purloined from Rothwell Town on the basis of him becoming a manager, although the Russians mainly wanted him as a player. He was a tremendous goal scorer, a manager who led by example and one hell of a character – which is the kindest way of describing him.

That very same season, 1963-64, the Diamonds were also champions. It was their fouth season in the Kettering and District Amateur League and they won it after they lost four out of their opening five matches. They didn't lose another game the whole season!

## RUSHDEN TOWN 1965-66

*L-r back: L. Camp, L. Pipes, T. Erskine, D. Williams, R. Allen, T Hawkesworth, P. DeBanke, B. Kirkup, R. Folwell, T. Murray (Manager)*
*L-r front: M. Walsh, A. Field, M. Dyte, B. Gilmour, M. Corbyn*

# The War Is Over – And Football Returns

Peter Martin took over from Don Mabelson as Player/Manager that season and Peter who had played for the youth team of the Diamonds and once scored 10 goals in a game (I can't remember who was the unfortunate team we played) was now a commanding centre half. He was also an excellent cricketer who later emigrated to Australia. I have seen him a couple of times in recent years and dined with him and his wife at Nene Park.

The 1964-65 season was remarkable for both clubs, but for entirely different reasons. The Russians, as reigning champions, were expecting more of the same but got a lot more than they bargained for. Not only did they finish a disastrous 9th out of 16 teams, they surrendered the crown back to Wellingborough Town, who incredibly thrashed the Russians 8-1. At the same time, Irthlingborough Diamonds changed league once again, applying for and getting elected to the United Counties League Division 2. They had been playing on the Recreation ground for 14 years but now the Irthlingborough council wanted to level the whole area.

Because of their poor timing and what I considered their bloody-mindedness, it meant that we would not be allowed to use the ground for a whole year! I had to beg the United Counties League committee to accept us on the basis that we use our regular dressing rooms at the Sow and Pigs Inn (The Oliver Twist) and instead of walking to the Recreation ground, we would lay on a coach (it turned out to be a double-decker bus), and transport both teams and officials a couple of miles up to the Welford Road estate where the council had another pitch.

How the UCL ever agreed to my request I will never know – but they did.

The Diamonds inauguration season as a UCL club saw them finished in a reasonable 6th spot. We were quietly pleased. The Diamonds were now only one league lower in status than their senior partners-to-be. The gap was closing. Within another two seasons it was to be closed altogether.

*1966. Irthlingborough Diamonds at the Recreation Ground.*
*L-r back: M. Nunn, J. Souster, M. Toms, G. Bosworth, M. Lloyd, I. McClellon, R. Byford. Front: K. Souter, M. Brown, D. Jones (Manager), B. Ellis, R. Manning.*

# Ten of Diamonds

1965-66 saw the Irthlingborough Diamonds finish three places higher in third position and they were back on the recreation ground all nicely levelled. In the same season, Rushden Town took part in what can only be described as one of the most bizarre league battles. How could a team score 154 goals in 36 games and not win the league?

Well, Rushden Town certainly did, with both Charlie Marlow and Mick Dyte each scoring over 50 goals – and they finished third behind champions Boston United! But the most remarkable statistic of all is that the top nine clubs all scored over one hundred goals each. Now that really is what I call attacking football!

The year of 1966 was the year of England's greatest football triumph but at a considerably lower level, history was being made in Irthlingborough. The Diamonds became United Counties League Division 2 champions under manager Dennis Jones, but the arch goal scorer was Barry Ellis, who, in all competitions of those three seasons, scored a staggering 200 goals!

Rushden Town finished 7th, proving yet again their inconsistency. What really concerned the Russians was not what had happened that season, but what might happen next. Their neighbours from Irthlingborough had caught them up at last. The following season, 1967-68, both Rushden Town and Irthlingborough Diamonds would be competing against each other in the same league on level terms for the first time ever.

It was a season that the boys of Irthlingborough were looking forward to with relish, and it was a season that the men of Rushden had been dreading for a long time.

# 3
# SUCCESS & FAILURE – IT'S A VERY THIN LINE

**THE DIAMONDS were now in the Division One of the United Counties League – they were still playing on the recreation ground, and every opposing team hated it.**

They were the worst facilities in the league, but at least we were no longer changing in a pub. We had convinced the local council to offer us the use of some new dressing rooms, which had primarily been built for the bowls section on the same ground.

At the end of a momentous season for the Diamonds, the club was delighted to finish 4th in their first season. This was the league and division which the Diamonds had been striving for, and now they were there, I figured that this is where they would stay forever and a day – how wrong can you be!

For Rushden Town, a 6th place finish would normally not be too bad, but to finish lower than the deadly enemy was totally unacceptable. St Neots were the champions that season, but as far as the Diamonds were concerned – they were.

The 1968-1969 season saw the Diamonds slip a couple of places down to 6th, but again, the Russians struggled, finishing one spot lower. In October '68, another Diamonds decision was reached – we were going to move yet again, but this time not into another league, but into a new home.

We considered that the club had outgrown the recreation ground and needed to move. It was not just a question of us having reached the UCL Division One and we wanted to be as smart as other clubs – although this was certainly true. It was because I was fed up with having stand-up battles with council groundsman Ted Peck and his surveyor boss Eric Phillpott, over the availability of the pitch. Every time it rained on a Friday night or Saturday morning, I was overcome with the inevitability of another row and yet one more game postponed.

Ted Peck was a cousin and supposed friend of my father, which counted for absolutely nothing. He was also the grandfather of Greg Peck who currently works at Nene Park as a security guard, steward and general factotum. Ted would argue that because the pitch had been re-seeded (that was a year earlier, for heaven's sake!), it needed careful handling – big deal!

My only concern was to play football on a football pitch – sounded pretty reasonable, I thought. But Ted always won the day. On arriving at the recreation ground at 10.00 in the morning, I would be met with a "Sorry Tony, too wet – match off." In just the same way that neighbours Rushden Town would be forced to look for a new ground some twenty years later (although for somewhat differing reasons), I decided enough was enough.

I opened up negotiations with the agents for Richard Thomas & Baldwin, who owned a field next to the Irthlingborough Cricket Club ground. It needed quite a lot of work doing to it to transform it into something resembling a football ground, but it was better than the

# Ten of Diamonds

constant arguments we were encountering.

Together with Robert Langley, I had more or less got a deal on the table when, out of the blue, I received a message which was to change our thinking and direction completely.

Councillor Reggie Bland, to whom I refer in another part of the book, was at an Irthlingborough council meeting and heard that the Mid-Northants Water Board was wanting to sell several acres of land off the A6, just on the outskirts of town. He asked another councillor, Don Rawlins, who was a friend of mine and lived only a few doors away, to call in my home and tell me of this possibility. All of the council were well aware of my arguments with their groundsman and were probably also fed up with my regular correspondence of complaints. Here was an opportunity to get me off their backs. I was immediately very interested.

We pulled out of the other land deal, and quickly got an agreement with the Water Board. They wanted to sell us the total area of their land but we couldn't afford it, and at the time, saw no need for it. So we purchased 5.6 acres at £200 per acre – we were now land-owners!

Some few years later we were able to buy an additional piece of adjoining land – another 3.3 acres, this time at £300 per acre. Unfortunately, there was a further few acres that we did not require or buy. More the pity, because in the early 1990's, the Griggs group paid a lot of money for this in the extended development, which now encompasses the Training Centre, car parking and pitch number three. Everything is so easy in retrospect.

Kuenen Brothers (later to become Pittards) were leather tanners and wanted to buy the building containing the pumping machinery so that they could extract water from the surrounding fields which are part of a water plain in the Nene Valley.

The building that was actually on our newly acquired piece of land was in two parts. One with the machinery, and the other empty and large, which was ideal for garaging all of our equipment. It was an arrangement that over the years worked very well.

In the autumn of 1968, the earth moving contractors moved in, ripping out a large hedge that grew right across the middle of the ground. Trees were also pulled up and suddenly there was a flat area – worthy of building a football stadium onto – which is the Nene Park of today.

Then the rain came.

So much so, that the seeding was delayed until the spring of 1969. In the spring, work began in earnest on the dressing rooms. We employed a single bricklayer, plus his labourer, and by summer the work was complete.

Peter Debanke, who had returned from playing football with Rushden Town after fourteen years, had come back to have a last swan song season with the Diamonds and then joined the committee. It was Peter who organised the gangs of voluntary workers – players, committee and anybody else who was prepared to help every weekend throughout the winter of 68/69, right through until the end of the summer, by which time the stand was completed. This included seating for 150 spectators, a good-sized standing area and a press box!

Builder and committee man John Underwood was particularly to the fore at

*Back l-r: Peter Debanke, Mel Lloyd.*
*Front: Cyril Jones, Robert Langley.*

28

# Success & Failure – It's a Very Thin Line

this time and a tremendous asset – so were many others. None more so than on a dreadfully bitter cold Sunday morning when the footings were to be dug out.

It was snowing hard and we had several guys in a three feet deep long trench digging away, while a pump was hammering away trying to keep the trench clear of water. Not only do I recall it well, but Peter Debanke took a cine-film (no videos in those days) of the incident.

Happy days! Yes, they actually were, because we were doing it all ourselves. There is no better satisfaction.

In the summer of '69, with father tending the pitch, all our thoughts turned to the new season and our opening day. On Wednesday 13th August, Nene Park opened for business. We were to play against a UCL Representative side, which included three from Bourne Town's championship side of the previous season, goalkeeper Glen Frost and Fred Patenall, both of Rushden Town. Charlie Marlow, ex-Rushden Town but now with the Desborough team, was captain, plus Dick Bushell, later to be an Irthlingborough Diamonds stalwart.

Ian Addis who for several years was a broadcaster on Radio Diamonds and a match day programme contributor, was also in the team. One of the current Rushden & Diamonds directors, namely Chris Smith, was in the home team, as was goal scorer extraordinaire Barry Ellis, who scored the first goal at the new ground. 3-3, it ended.

In the souvenir programme, my father, who was chairman at the time, thanked the FA and particularly the Irthlingborough Urban District Council for their loans which enabled us to complete the project at a cost of approximately £8,000!

The other interesting scenario and problem that we initially had to overcome was that of access from the A6 highway, onto the slip road and into the ground. Whereas access today is via the large roundabout – which came some 25 years later – the entrance was where today, entry is only available to emergency vehicles!

Because the local council were very anxious to see us re-located, the surveyor Eric Phillpott suddenly became a considerable help. He had to get the Department of Transport Inspector to come down to look at the access situation which was proving to be a major stumbling block. Eric tipped me off that the gentleman in question had been a keen footballer in his day for Bishop Auckland. We looked, we talked and then went to the 'Railway Inn' just a few yards away (long since demolished), and talked again.

I laid it on thick – he would be the one guy to bring our whole project crashing down – and him being an ex-footballer! He didn't like the access off the A6 one little bit – but said OK!

Our opening UCL game at Nene Park was on Sunday 17th August 1969. We chose a Sunday for maximum local interest and beat Desborough Town 3-1, with Peter Garley scoring the first ever league goal at Nene Park. By the end of the season, Bourne Town were champions yet again, but Rushden Town reversed the previous seasons battle-royale by finishing third and the Diamonds fourth.

Now that the Diamonds were nicely settled in their own little stadium, we wanted more of the action. The real action in footballing parlance can mean only one thing – a championship winning team.

Now was the time to make our mark, although Chris Smith had by now jumped ship, I really believed we could overtake Rushden Town in the local popularity stakes. We had the impetus within us, so let's go for it.

In the summer leading up to the start of the 1970-71 season, we made key signings. Midfielder John Adams, who had played in the Bourne Town championship side, was acquired. This was to prove vital.

However the real 'icing on the cake' came following my pursuit of Northampton Spencer hard man Dick Bushell. He could play centre half, full back or mid field and was a player who should have played in the Football League. He was excellent.

I invited him to my home for tea and negotiations. I picked him up in Northampton

# Ten of Diamonds

*Dick Bushell*

where I was working, and my wife did the rest. Dick ate the biggest meal imaginable, "Splendid!", he said, or something like that. Then I produced my ace card – a car.

It was to be a pale blue Austin A40, and Ken Ambridge, my counterpart at Rushden Town, told me only recently that despite my insistence on secrecy, they all knew about it and were livid that those bloody Diamonds were splashing out in this manner to get the best players! Bit ironic that, because Rushden Town's Cyril Freeman, some forty years earlier, had been tempting players from the North East to join them and later, Ted Duckhouse had a house provided for him.

Anyway, Dick Bushell became the catalyst for other signings from Northampton Spencer as the season got underway. Barry Shellswell, or "Shells" as he was commonly known, was either a centre forward or a left winger – needless to say, he was all left foot, but he could play. I convinced him to join us quite early on in the season – thank goodness he couldn't drive!

Once Dick Bushell knew that we had clinched the signing of "Shells", he told me that Spencer had a right winger, Peter Phipps, who was even better. One viewing was enough – 'Phippy' was my next target. However, there was a problem. As amateurs, a seven-day notice of approach was required, and although we knew 'Phippy' wanted to join us, the Diamonds could not approach the same club (Spencer) for another thirty days,

I already had two of their best players and now wanted a third – sooner rather than later. So Peter Phipps had to tell Spencer that he had approached us and he had this desire to join this up-and-coming club at Irthlingborough. This way, Spencer couldn't stop him, but all hell broke loose. Brian Faulkner was the Spencer manager – a tough, no nonsense adversary. He rightly raised the roof, reported us to the Northants F.A and to the F.A in London.

Dick's involvement and rumours about his car were rife. I told him to deny everything and he did. The fracas continued throughout the season. Meanwhile, Shells and Phippy's attacking flair set the Diamonds alight but there was still another problem – Rothwell Town.

Rothwell had slugged it out, toe to toe with us all season, and the last match of the season was – you've guessed it – Rothwell v Diamonds at Cecil Street. The Diamonds had only to draw while Rothwell had to win, and a record UCL crowd of over 2,500 came for the showdown. Our centre-half, Barry Alexander, headed us into the lead before a Rothwell equaliser early in the second half. With two minutes remaining, Barry Shelswell put Mick Toms away and he lobbed the keeper from so far out that the ball took ages to reach the line. It's the only time we appreciated the massive slope on their pitch

We were champions of the UCL for the first time of our four league titles. However, the Barry Shelswell story doesn't end there. On a snowy Boxing Day match at Hayden Road against our old rivals Rushden Town, 'Shells' went missing.

He just didn't turn up. I later found out that he was still in bed recovering from a bad Christmas hangover. Although I

*Barry Shelswell*

# Success & Failure – It's a Very Thin Line

was furious, I covered for him with some 'cock and bull' story and he rejoined the team at the next game without anyone the wiser. I reminded him of it when I saw him recently. He says he couldn't remember!

Another side story to that fateful Boxing Day was that the Russians won 4-1 with a certain Rushden & Diamonds director, Chris Smith, scoring for them. As for 'Shells', his presence throughout the rest of the season was critical, but also the Diamonds commenced a ten-year run of consecutive success. On the night of the Championship victory over Rothwell, we celebrated long and hard at The Horseshoe pub in Irthlingborough. We had no clubhouse at the time but wanted to carry on with the fun at the ground; by now we were well and truly inebriated (I've always used posh words).

I drove my car full of players to Nene Park, with Barry Shelswell sitting on the bonnet. Anyway, car after car turned up including all the wives and girlfriends. We switched on the floodlights on the training area (there weren't any on the pitch at this stage), which thank goodness were of mediocre standard. I say that because the girls also stripped down to their underwear and boys v girls was definitely good fun.

The training pitch was right next to the A6 trunk road and considering it was around midnight, it wasn't long before the police came. We explained that we had just won the league and this was just a continuation of our celebrations. They were fine about it, congratulated us and left as quickly as they had come.

Our moment of glory had been wonderfully invigorating but we now knew that up the road, the Russians would be determined to reverse the roles next time around.

Furthermore, last season's champions, Bourne Town, and this season's runners-up, Rothwell, would be after our blood and wouldn't let the new kids on the block do it again.

We knew that from now on, it could only get tougher.

Nothing was more certain than the Russians hitting back immediately. They were in no mood to be surpassed by the so-called amateurs on the other side of the Nene. However, it was Bourne Town, under the leadership of the no-nonsense Terry Bates, who triumphed by claiming their third UCL title in four years. If Rushden Town couldn't quite win it, then finishing second and above third place Diamonds was almost as good.

The following season, the Russians went one better and became the UCL champions for the first time since 1964, winning by six points from Spalding with the Diamonds slipping further back into 5th place. Now the smiles were back at Hayden Road, and none more so than on the face of ex-Diamond Chris Smith, who netted 36 league goals that season.

However, in the next season '73/'74', neither the Diamonds nor Rushden Town had anything to smile about. Inexplicably both clubs slid down the league dramatically, with the Russians just pipping the Diamonds to 10th place! It was time for reflection and some new faces, but the form of both clubs only improved marginally with Diamonds in 5th place and Rushden Town up to 8th position. Chris Smith, who had rejoined Diamonds that season netted 41 goals and missed 12 games! However, the so-called dream partnership with Peter Phipps and Howard Kettleborough who had joined from Hitchin Town never really functioned, mainly because of injuries to one or another of them.

The 1976-77 season saw a cliff-hanger finish with the league only decided in the dying seconds of the season.

Going into the last game, Stamford held a one point lead over the Diamonds. Bearing in mind that in those days, a win only received two points, so even if the Diamonds won their home game against Desborough Town (which they did 3-0), Stamford only had to get a draw at rock-bottom Vauxhall Motors because of their superior goal average (not goal difference).

With our game at Nene Park safely in the bag and with only minutes remaining, I telephoned Vauxhall Motors anticipating the worst.

"It's 3-3.......no, wait a minute.....a goal has just been scored!", said the lady on the other end. "Oh damn", I exclaimed, thinking it was Stamford. "Who's scored?" I hardly dare ask.

# Ten of Diamonds

"Vauxhall Motors", she said, quite nonchalantly.

"Are you absolutely certain?", I asked again.

"Of course. And the game has just ended", she replied.

My old pal David Knighton was standing next to me and he immediately announced the score over the tannoy. Amazingly, our players just stopped playing and Desborough's sat down and waited for the jubilation to settle.

The ref decided to blow for time and then the real party started.

\*       \*       \*       \*       \*

In the period of eight years up to 1983, Irthlingborough Diamonds and Stamford dominated the UCL totally. Whilst Diamonds had three championship titles, Stamford were even more successful, claiming the championship five times!

The year of 1978 was perhaps equal in importance to their 1969 ground acquisition. The decision to have floodlights was in itself an exciting occasion and I was determined to again put one over on my buddy Ken Ambridge at Hayden Road. Sure enough, by November, we were ready for the big switch-on.

Although Kettering Town, in a higher league, had good floodlights, Wellingborough Town was the only other team in the county outside of the Cobblers to have them and theirs were not a very good standard. All I wanted was to be ahead of Rushden Town, who had apparently been thinking about them for quite a while.

A game was fixed against a so-called All-Stars team for November 28th and through an intermediary, we were able to make contact with Bobby Robson who was then manager

*L-r: Tony Jones with Bobby Robson (Ipswich Town Manager) pull the switches for the opening of the floodlights at the original Nene Park. November 1978.*

# Success & Failure – It's a Very Thin Line

at Ipswich Town, to come along and officially switch on the floodlights. He told me that he would bring along one of his first team players to play in the game. That was a real bonus!

However, circumstances intervened to somewhat spoil the occasion.

A couple of weeks earlier we had a rather surprising draw, 0-0 at Dagenham in the 4th Qualifying Round of the FA Cup, and therefore a replay had to take place at Nene Park. The floodlights were ready, so why not use them, even if it meant playing under them a week before the official inauguration.

This we did, and although losing 2-1 we had our record gate of 2560 to compensate. The winners had been drawn away to Watford and this possibility for a UCL minnow would have been the big time.

A week later, Bobby Robson did the official business and the player he brought with him was Brian Talbot.

Our manager Tony Sabey pulled off a coup by getting Brian to turn out for the Diamonds, so it can be recorded that Brian made his debut for the Diamonds back in 1978! After the game, Brian said to me that if we won the league he would be pleased to come along and present the trophies at the end of the season.

*Tony Sabey*

We finished as champions with Rushden Town as runners-up and I was anxious to make contact with Mr Talbot as soon as possible. In the January of 1979, Brian had been transferred to Arsenal, so I telephoned Highbury and spoke to him.

"Of course I'll come", said Brian

*George Whiting*

The Civic Hall in Irthlingborough, now boarded up and looking very sorry for itself, was decked out beautifully. "The Diamonds welcome Brian Talbot", read the large banner fixed to the wall and good to his promise, he presented all the trophies. That weekend, Brian stayed at my house and from that day some 24 years ago, we have been close friends.

Two seasons later, Roger Ashby took over as player/manager when Tony Sabey decided to call it a day. Roger's team had a new look about it and Joe Kiernan of ex-Cobblers fame became his assistant.

George Whiting was another newcomer to the Diamonds, and became Club Secretary in 1981 and remained in the position until the merger in 1992, when he was cruelly passed over for a senior position in the new club. George was a complete workaholic and I admired his tremendous enthusiasm and energy. In later years

# Ten of Diamonds

he organised, but more importantly, attended every Sunday morning car boot sale, arriving at Nene Park at 5.30am together with David Joyce, who ironically was to replace him as Secretary of Rushden & Diamonds.

*Irthlingborough Diamonds Team plus four cups.*

The league form of both Diamonds and Rushden Town was mediocre, finishing in 9th and 7th spots respectively, but it was the Diamonds' season for grabbing the headlines in cup competitions. They won the NFA Senior Cup, the UCL Knock-Out Cup, the Hinchingbrooke Cup and the Wellingborough Charity Cup. However their real claim to fame was in the F.A. Vase.

In the 6th round, the Diamonds drew 0-0 away to Basildon and in the replay at Nene Park, were losing 4-2 with five minutes remaining. Fans were leaving the ground when the Diamonds dramatically scored twice to equalise and two more in extra time to win 6-4. Steve Birch bagged four goals that day and became a legend in FA Vase history.

Sadly, the two-leg semi-final didn't live up to the previous thriller and after drawing 1-1 at Nene Park, we lost 2-0 at Willenhall.

In the October of 1982 a bad fire ruined the Diamonds clubhouse but at least it gave us the opportunity to smarten the place up. It's quite surprising what a good insurance policy can do.

The 1982-1983 season was to be Rushden Town's last in the UCL. They finished as runners-up again that season but the Irthlingborough Diamonds were the champions again.

The FA introduced their new pyramid system throughout their non-league football in England. This would be the last time that clubs would be able to change league of their own choice.

# Success & Failure – It's a Very Thin Line

Rushden Town saw this as a good opportunity to advance themselves and break away from the Diamonds and they were elected to the Midland Division of the Southern League. We had the same chance to do likewise but although some of my colleagues wanted to follow Rushden, I was concerned about finances and we declined.

It is an interesting thought that had we done so, then the fact that we would have been in a higher league than the UCL when Max Griggs took over – it would have possibly remained as Irthlingborough Diamonds, who would have then been in the Football League today – not Rushden & Diamonds.

Such are the quirks of fate.

Rushden Town's first adventures in their new competition saw them finish a creditable 7th whilst the Diamonds failed miserably also in the same slot in the UCL. However their exploits kept them on the map again with another FA Vase semi-final against their arch rivals Stamford Town. Losing the first leg at Nene Park 2-1 was not their idea of fun and sure enough Stamford won well in the second leg 2-0 to go back to Wembley where they triumphed splendidly.

The 1984-1985 saw the Russians in turmoil. In December 1984 they decided to apply for re-election to the UCL due to financial problems. Consequently, the manager Mick Walpole and assistant Steve Wisman (both ex Diamonds players) walked out of the club in disgust at the committee's decision. Wages were cut, several players joined the exodus and Jeff Redding (of Irthlingborough's Central Garage) became the new manager. They finished the season in 13th spot but decided after all to stay with the Southern League.

Two years later they finished bottom, only winning one game and conceding 124 goals. The club was in real crisis. Meanwhile the Diamonds kept chugging along, finishing in fourth position in three consecutive years. The major change at Nene Park saw Roger Ashby resign on a point of principle and Chris Smith took over the reigns.

The 87-88 season at Hayden Road started disastrously. 48 year old John Daldy took up the poisoned chalice as manager and promptly played in all the games before he was replaced. The Russians were slaughtered at Merthyr Tyfhil 11-0, fielding a team of local amateurs and youngsters, and then Roger Ashby took up the challenge. He made important signings like Billy Jeffrey who was later to join him with Rushden & Diamonds as his assistant and Andy Kirkup who later became a fan's favourite at Nene Park.

The change in personnel had such a marked effect that in the return game at Hayden Road, Merthyr were put to the sword by three goals to one as the Russians finished the season in 15th position – a great turn around under the circumstances.

Meanwhile at Irthlingborough, the Diamonds were sliding into trouble. They finished 13th in the UCL and their glory days were over. However on a very personal note, tragedy struck home at the Diamonds.

David Knighton died from cancer in early 1988. He had been ill for several months and it was on the day of our best win of the seasons, beating Southern League club Buckingham Town 4-0 at Nene Park, that David came to my house a couple of hours before the game and told me that he only had a few months to live.

Incredibly, in between that day and when he passed away three months later, he single-handedly organised a very special 'This Is Your Life' evening at the club for my father and myself. It marked a 40-year period with the Diamonds and was a total surprise for both of us, having been secreted to the club on a totally ambiguous story. David had contacted over 100 old players, some dating all the way back to 1947. It was a wonderful evening but a very poignant one also. All of us were aware of the circumstances surrounding David's health and the fact that he was brave enough to host the whole ceremony only highlights what a great guy he was.

I miss him dearly even now, and talk of him often.

1988-1989 was a moderate season for both clubs but a year later, while Diamonds were languishing in 12th place in the UCL, Rushden Town hit the promotion hot-spot by finishing

# Ten of Diamonds

runners-up to Halesowen and securing their place in the Southern League Premier Division for 1990-1991.

Roger Ashby had done brilliantly in his two seasons at Hayden Road, completely changing the club around. It was somewhat ironic that having left the Diamonds due to internal problems, that he should reappear at Rushden Town and take them into a new league which was two leagues higher.

Meanwhile the Diamonds were facing a crisis. Problems everywhere! Shortage of money, committed people and enthusiasm was now very evident. The club was in free-fall and I really didn't know what to do about it.

The 1989-1990 season we were 12th in the league and the following year even lower in 14th spot. Chris Smith had tried to halt the slide with a short second term as manager but soon handed over to Paul Brackwell who was then quickly dismissed. Gary Savage had the job for a few months then suffered the same fate.

Rushden Town's one and only season in the Premier Division of the Southern League proved equally dramatic.

They finished 14th in the final table but the real bad news came after they had thrashed Chelmsford 6-1. The Southern League confirmed that the club would be relegated back into the Midland Division due to their ground not conforming to the standard required. It was a very sad day for the Russians, having strived so hard to reach the higher grade only to see it snatched away from them in this manner. The major concern was that their wooden stand was deemed to be dangerous. They had been aware of the problem for some time but all efforts to obtain a ground they could own had unfortunately failed.

Roger Ashby, speaking to the Evening Telegraph at that time said, "This means that Rushden Town has played its last game at this level at Hayden Road. So unless a new venue is found quickly, Rushden Town Football Club can only go one way – down and finally out. The Chairman, Neil Gant, has backed me to the hilt and to walk away from that would be difficult. But having said that, I'm very ambitious and want to manage at the highest possible level".

Roger, nor anyone else, could have ever foreseen what was to happen under twelve months later.

1991-1992 was to be the final season for both Irthlingborough Diamonds and Rushden Town.

The Diamonds had a dreadful season fielding youngsters and players who would have struggled to get into their reserve teams during their heyday. They finished 17th in the league – their lowest ever position. Meanwhile the Russians, having completed their league fixtures by finishing 8th, played their last ever game at Hayden Road on May 12th 1992 against Leighton Town in the final of the South Midlands Floodlight Cup, which they won 4-2.

I was present at that game, which normally would have been somewhat unusual but as we were soon to become brothers in the summer then this was not considered strange by the few fans who witnessed the end of a fine club of over 100 years standing. They had been a senior club in the county all this time. They had enjoyed immense success.

But now it was all over.

A merger was the only answer!

# 4
# I WANT NENE PARK TO BE A FUN PLACE

Chairman Max Griggs made it clear from the outset what his vision was for the club. He said, "I want Nene Park to be a fun place and a family place. That's the way to build something for the future".

And that is exactly what the next ten years proved to be.

Well, perhaps there were times when the word 'fun' could be questioned, but a decade is a long time for everything to be as perfect as one would like.

August 22nd 1992 was the all-important date. The Southern League Midland Division fixtures had been received and Bilston at Nene Park was our opener. They were an old established West Midland club and although they would be a firm test, we quietly fancied our chances.

The Board and the newly joined-together committee had done everything we considered possible to capture the mood of the local population. But were the fans of the Russians actually going to cross the river to watch a new club with only half their name in it? Would the small band of Diamonds supporters continue to support a club which had 'Rushden' as a prefix? And probably more importantly, could we attract a completely new section of followers?

We hoped so, but still didn't know. We circulated all the schools in Rushden, Higham and Irthlingborough with leaflets, urging them and their parents to come along and see what we were all on about.

In truth, we hadn't got a lot to offer. The facilities, although improved to meet league requirements, were very little different from the original Diamonds. The team would obviously be stronger but so was the league in which we were competing. We made special arrangements for a coach to pick up at various points in Rushden and transport fans to Nene Park.

There was little else we could do. As it transpired, 315 supporters were attracted, which was at least double compared to when Rushden Town played the same team the previous season. This was one way of consoling ourselves, but we were somewhat disappointed, nonetheless.

The match itself was not very good – which is one way of describing it – and I suppose a 2-2 draw was about right. As a point of interest to the readers who like recorded history, the Rushden & Diamonds team was Kevin Shoemake, Mark Bushell, Junior Wilson, Darrell Page, John Flower, Dave Johnson, Steve Heard, Adie Mann, Ollie Kearns, Frankie Belfon and Paul York. The goalscorers in this inaugural league game were Ollie Kearns and Frankie Belfon, with old stager Ollie becoming another 'first' in the annals of Nene Park.

# TEN OF DIAMONDS

Three draws mean three points and that was the sum total of the Diamonds' opening trio of games played by the end of August. Glenville Donegal, who had started his career with the Cobblers but had last played with Maidstone United, (then in administration), was signed and scored in the first game, a 2-1 home win over Bridgnorth. I particularly remember the 2nd qualifying round of the F.A Cup which we won 1-0 against Long Buckby, not because of Donegal's lone winner, but because I was recovering at home following the wedding ceremony of my daughter Alison, to Peter Clarke, our centre-half of Irthlingborough Diamonds, the previous day.

We had held the reception in a marquee in my garden and the aftermath was such that even me, the keenest of the keen, couldn't draw up enough enthusiasm to travel to Long Buckby! The date is memorable, obviously for the wedding, but also for the most dramatic and tragic of reasons nine years later.

It was September 11th – 1992 and 2001.

By the middle of November, seven more league games were under our belt and the season was not going quite according to our own declared script. Two wins, three draws and two defeats add up to only nine points from a potential twenty one, and the gates were mainly in the two hundreds – yuck! One month later, and the smiles were slowly returning – four wins on the trot and twelve goals scored against two conceded was more like it. Right-winger Andy Kirkup had notched the first hat-trick for the club in a 5-0 win against Evesham United and repeated the feat four weeks later against Kings Lynn, winning 3-1.

*Dale Watkins*

Back in November, on a wet windy evening, Grantham Town had been well beaten 4-1 at Nene Park, but a very quick small guy had been very impressive for the visitors. His name was Dale Watkins and by early 1993, he was a Diamonds player. Right on cue, Dale opened with a hat-trick in a 6-0 home drubbing of Hinckley Town. He was to score nearly one hundred more before moving onto Gloucester City a few years later.

Five wins and a draw saw us moving quickly up the league – the draw being a 1-1 at the champion elect Nuneaton, so the camp was a happy one. After a 4-1 beating at Tamworth, the club started to believe it could reach either of the top two spots needed for promotion with a blistering six consecutive victories.

Defeats by Barri (Barry Town by another moniker but at loggerheads with the Welsh FA) and then Nuneaton at Nene Park badly dented our hopes of immediate elevation. To make matters worse, a 1-0 defeat followed at Leicester United.

Nevertheless, a tremendous finishing burst worthy of a top sprinter saw the Diamonds take nineteen points from their last seven league matches and finish a very creditable third behind Nuneaton Borough and Gresley Rovers in the first league table.

During the season, Chairman Max Griggs announced that a new 1000-seater stand would be erected and ready for the next season. Work started on February 1993 with John Sayer of Laser Management Construction being given the go-ahead to build.

Now we were really starting to look the part. I well remember the club director Robert Langley debating with Max as to the viability and need for a 1000-seater when our average

## I Want Nene Park to be a Fun Place

gate turned out to be 318 – only three more than our opening league game of the season. However Max was very confident that once the fans saw what was being provided, they would come – and they did. Nevertheless, I can't say I was anywhere near as confident at the time. He proved us wrong then, and did so again on later projects.

*Irthlingborough Diamonds clubhouse is quickly demolished.*

"You must believe", said Max.

The summer of 1993 at Nene Park was quite breathtaking. Not only was Max's dream, 1000-seater sparkling and in situ, but the old Irthlingborough Diamonds stand, dressing rooms, boardroom and clubhouse had all been demolished – gone!

It was these same facilities which, together with my colleagues some 24 years earlier, we had lovingly built, if not entirely with our own hands, certainly in kind and spirit.

I was told when the large JCB would be in action and on that very morning, I witnessed the carnage. Surprisingly enough to my friends who knew of my presence – I felt no regrets. In fact, it was exciting. That was then and this is now. It was the beginning of a new era. I was beginning to believe that Max's dream of Conference football in five years could be more than just a dream. I didn't think so when it was first mentioned but I was catching on – fast.

At the end where the Peter Debanke terrace now stands with the car park behind it, there was just a wire mesh fence and the grass training ground behind it.

Well, there was - until that summer.

Portacabins sprung up and down that side, providing offices, temporary dressing rooms and a hospitality room. A relocated ground entrance led to a splendid newly laid pitch and to really set the ground alight, were superb new high floodlights towering over the NEW NENE PARK.

The man really meant business!

But it got even better. Max had been made aware of Millwall wanting to sell their electronic scoreboard at the Old Den. They were moving to a new ground barely a mile away, but as far as the Millwall fans were concerned, it could have been a million miles. On the last Saturday of the season, the fans completely wrecked the stadium. Max, Mark Darnell and myself had an appointment at the Old Den on the following Monday morning. Hundreds of seats had been ripped out and thrown everywhere – it was a disaster zone. Max subsequently bought their scoreboard, and the Millwall fans moved down the road and never gave the old stadium a second thought.

# TEN OF DIAMONDS

*BEFORE*  *AFTER*

*Irthlingborough Diamonds main stand*

*Mickey Nuttell*

That's how fickle football can be.

All three strikers who had started the previous season were gone by the start of this one. The new 1993-94 season saw Donegal off to Australia – I've heard of being sent to Coventry, but 'down under' is a bit much.

Frankie Belfon took a much shorter journey to Northampton Spencer while Ollie Kearns was simply well past his best and just left. This only left Dale Watkins who had looked lively but in need of a good big guy's help.

He found it in Mickey Nuttell, who was to prove an excellent signing and the goalscorer we needed. He also had the distinction of scoring the first goal – albeit in a friendly against Northampton Town – in front of a packed new North Stand. "Where was Robert Langley now?", mused Max.

The other key signing was ex-Poppy, Paul Richardson, a battling mid-fielder from Dagenham and Redbridge. Alan Kurila, brother of Irthlingborough Diamonds striker

## I Want Nene Park to be a Fun Place

Mick, who had broken his leg in a pre-season friendly, was another addition, joining from Burton Albion.

We were off to a flyer.

The first eight league games registered six wins and two draws, in which Nuttell netted on seven occasions. Added to this, we had five early FA Cup games of which four were won, with one draw. In the same period up to the end of October, three wins and a draw in the Dr Martens League KO Cup had given the club a dream start.

The only downside was a 1-0 home defeat to Southern League Premier Division Burton Albion in the F.A Trophy, to which we had been upgraded from the previous year in the F.A Vase.

Ironically, this was a competition with more chance of success whereas in the F.A Cup 3rd Qualifying Round we had beaten the same Burton Albion 4-0.

Such are the vagaries of football.

After our tremendous start and with attendance double last season, it was particularly disappointing to lose 3-2 at home to lowly Hinckley Town – a team we were to beat on their own ground 4-0 later that season. Nevertheless, it was a wake-up call and both Bilston Town and Tamworth fell heavily under the hammer at Nene Park, both beaten 5-1.

It was not until January 29th 1994 that we lost another league match to Weston Super Mare, 2-1. Since the Hinckley defeat, we had enjoyed a 12-match unbeaten league run, winning nine of them. By this time, Nuttell and Watkins were scoring for fun. I remember the trip to Weston Super Mare very well. It was one of the first occasions that we had stayed overnight but I can't say that I will be spurning Spain for Weston when it comes to choice of holidays.

If we thought that twelve consecutive games without defeats was good – then how about twenty games!

On February 5th, we beat Yate Town 3-0 at Nene Park and then had this incredible run right through to the end of the season. Added to that run was an NFA Senior Cup Semi-Final Victory over Conference neighbours Kettering Town, by 3-2 at Nene Park, played in front of 2,352 spectators. A great performance, and a great gate.

The final of that competition was anti-climactic, thrashing Northampton Spencer 5-0, but who cared – Dale Watkins certainly didn't as he weighed in with another hat trick. After the NFA Senior Cup final had been played, we had three matches, all played at Nene Park, to finish off our league programme and hopefully beat V.S Rugby to the title.

We were now getting over 1000 gates as the season reached its climax.

The first of these last three home games was against Evesham United. We had won 4-1 at Evesham earlier in the year so would there be a problem? You bet there would – and it came in the towering figure of a young keeper named Billy Turley. He stopped everything. Well, almost.

We had outplayed Evesham and on another day might have had a hat full but an Adie Mann goal was all Turley was prepared to concede. An interesting twist to this story occurred a few weeks later when Mr Turley senior telephoned me, asking whether we would like to sign his son Billy. I passed the message on to Roger Ashby, who said "No, he's too young".

That decision was to cost the club £100,000 some five years later when we signed him from Northampton Town. Four days after Evesham came Forest Green Rovers and victory for the Diamonds meant we were the champions. Over 1500 spectators came to Nene Park on an evening when for some obscure reason, the kick-off was scheduled for 7.00. We had fine floodlights so there was no problem there, but as circumstances turned out, I thank goodness we did kick off early.

We were leading 3-0 on the hour – everything going according to plan – when out went the lights!

Help was soon to hand, but to no avail. I told secretary Dave Joyce to quickly tell the referee that the lights would be on very shortly. "Just keep stalling him", I said to Dave.

# Ten of Diamonds

*John Flower collects the Southern League, Midland Division Trophy.*

He did once more, by which time the natural light was fading fast. We scored twice more to make it 5-0, but would we finish? With five minutes still to go to the final whistle, it was virtually dark, but by this time, the referee couldn't possibly abandon it – and didn't.

The championship was ours. The fans raced onto the pitch and the floodlights burst into action. Voila!

Without the mysterious 7.00pm kick-off, the game would never have been finished, and who knows what would have happened in a replay? The celebrations for the first championship of the new club Rushden & Diamonds followed in real style.

But there was still one more game to play. I remember talking to a Redditch official in the week and he said something like, "Well, don't expect to beat US by 5-0!"

We didn't – we thrashed them 7-0, the best finale possible before almost 1400 fans.

The gates on average had trebled compared with the previous season and Max's comments that if you give the fans top-class facilities to go alongside a winning team, then you've got a successful formula.

He was right again!

During the season, the chairman had allowed Roger Ashby to buy Dougie Keast for £3,000 from Corby Town and our mid-field improved immediately. He also permitted the signing of Paul Coe from Cambridge City for £10,000. This was big money for an outside-left who usually flattered to deceive. He never appeared to settle or believe that he belonged. Before the following season he had returned to his former club for a similar fee, having scored only four goals in his 23 league appearances. Goals win matches and lots of goals win championships, and so it proved.

The strike force of Mickey Nuttell and Dale Watkins were just too hot to handle, scoring 73 goals between them in all competitions. In the league, Nuttell netted 29 from 40 games, while Watkins scored 23 from the same number of matches.

In winning the Midland Division Championship, 109 goals were scored and 98 points acquired. This was 6 points more than V.S Rugby who were also promoted to the Premier Division. Weston –Super-Mare missed out by just one point.

The Premier Division of the Southern League beckoned – we had everything to play for.

# 5
# FULL STEAM AHEAD

**CHAIRMAN MAX now had the bit between his teeth and deemed that the summer of '94 would be full steam ahead at Nene Park.**

The promotion to Premier Division of the Southern League only served as an additional spur to his expansive (and expensive) creation. Nene Park was alive that summer with preparations for the new West Terrace well underway. Gone were the portacabins that had been erected only a year before, with the new dressing rooms under the splendid South Stand ready for use at the start of the '94-'95 season.

*The Board Room at Nene Park*

The South Stand and adjoining Diamond Centre was complete. One can only describe the facilities and the quality as nothing short of magnificent. The marble entrance and stairway to the Diamond Centre, together with an incredible giant-sized chandelier simply mirrored Max's vision. He wanted the best.

# Ten of Diamonds

A boardroom overlooking the pitch, a function room for 200 guests, a smaller room catering for half that number and three hospitality corporate suites – and that was on the first floor!

On the ground floor, were the dressing rooms leading directly out onto the pitch, office accommodation, the club's archives containing memorabilia from the original clubs and a public bar that would have graced any hotel. In fact all the facilities were of a standard that had not been seen at any other football club in the country outside of perhaps the top Premiership clubs, and even that was debatable.

Before the actual opening of the Centre, we had to decide on names for the various function rooms and bars. We agreed on Kimberley for our most capacious room, in line with the South African diamond mine. The other function area became the 'Sparklers' whilst the large bar was originally known as 'Trumps'. All of these names had connections with the Diamonds and that was our general theme thinking at the time. We deviated however from this association when naming the hospitality suites and these became the Manton, Hayden and Chichele.

The 'Manton' was a reminder of where the original Irthlingborough Diamonds played most of their football at the Manton Road recreation ground.

The 'Hayden' was from the old Hayden Road ground where the Rushden team had enjoyed and witnessed so many of their glory days. It is still there today, used by the various youth teams of Rushden Rangers and although the old stand has been drastically reduced in size, it is still a poignant reminder of the halcyon days of the old Russians.

So naming those two suites was comparatively easy but what about the third one? We were uncertain regarding this but eventually settled for 'Chichele' as nobody at the time could come up with anything better.

So who, or what, was Chichele?

The small town of Higham Ferrers links Rushden to Irthlingborough by virtue of the A6 trunk road and Henry Chichele was born the son of a farmer in Higham Ferrers in 1362.

He was educated at Winchester and Oxford and went on to become the Archbishop of Canterbury in 1414, eventually dying in 1443 aged 81 years. Always remembering his birthplace, he founded the Bede House and college, the derelict walls of which still stand to this day in the High Street. It is referred to by locals as the Chichele College. As with the 'Trumps' bar which we later renamed 'Strikers', perhaps somebody one day may think of a more deserving or associated name – but that's for another day.

Whilst still on the subject of names, I mentioned that the West Terrace was started at that time and the board of directors unanimously accepted my suggestion of the Peter Debanke Terrace. It was to be an all-standing area, where over the following years, the real hard core of our fans would gather.

As I have stated earlier in the book, Peter was one of the originals of the old Irthlingborough Diamonds from the age of 13. He played only in Youth football for the Diamonds until he returned some 20 years later at the end of his playing career.

In between times, he played for Rushden Town for fourteen consecutive seasons, was captain for a lot of the time and had the incredible record of never having been booked during a match! I always joked with him that it was because he never tackled, but that just wasn't true.

Once he was back with the Diamonds and his playing days were over, Peter came onto the committee and really was Commander-in-Chief of our grand building operations. In addition, he helped manager Dennis Jones with training two nights a week and when Dennis left the club, Peter formed a dual partnership with Mel Lloyd, which resulted in our first ever UCL championship. He later assisted Tony Sabey on the management side and another UCL trophy came to Nene Park.

He was the complete all-rounder.

## Full Steam Ahead

Now you know why it's called the Peter Debanke Terrace.

As if all the activity at the stadium wasn't enough, the playing side was similarly being revamped. Whilst Roger Ashby thought that he had the good nucleus of players from his Midland Division winning squad, he was nevertheless aware of certain shortcomings.

He needed a classy hard-working midfield player and a strong running goalscoring striker. He could never have chosen better.

Midfielder Garry Butterworth was signed from Dagenham & Redbridge for a tribunal fixed fee of £22,000 and was a bargain and a half!

Garry lived in Peterborough and therefore our location suited him much better, and he was to become the longest serving player in the club's history, making a total number of 371 appearances – but that's for later.

Darren Collins, a £20,000 transfer from Enfield, also made club history by scoring a total 153 goals for the club before he left six years later. So there were two major signings and yet another indication of the Chairman's desire and intent.

Darren had been with Northampton Town for three seasons, appearing in the first team on 68 occasions but something was obviously missing – maybe the final desire, but it certainly wasn't the ability. He was strong, pacy and could score goals with either foot – he was exactly what we needed.

Ironically, it was in a pre-season friendly that Darren signalled his intentions with a two-goal salvo against none other than the Cobblers. Over 2,000 spectators witnessed it and by now we were all getting very excited.

*Garry Butterworth*

*Darren Collins celebrates his goal.*

# Ten of Diamonds

By virtue of having won the NFA Senior Cup the previous season, we were now scheduled to entertain Peterborough United in a one-off game for the NFA Mansell Cup at Nene Park. Goals from Mickey Nuttell and Dale Watkins saw the Diamonds carry off the magnificent trophy 2-1 against the Football League club and now the excitement was turning into anticipation – that of another promotion.

How that optimism was to be dented was immediately evident.

Cheltenham Town, who over the next few years were to become the bane of our lives, beat us 2-0 in our opening game at Nene Park in front of 1,610 supporters. Captain John Flower, who was a tough, uncompromising central defender, was always likely to catch the attention of referees, who were now working under new tighter guidelines, and so it proved. He was dismissed for a cynical foul and we could never thereafter get to grips with our opponents.

Even so, four wins and a draw quickly followed with Dale Watkins scoring five times and Darren Collins on four occasions – this was more like it.

Having said that, our FA Cup aspirations ended abysmally at Eastwood Hanley in early September, losing 1-0 to a club no one had ever heard of – they had now! Added to this woe, we stumbled over the next four league games, losing three of them; away to old rivals Gresley Rovers and Dorchester Town, together with another disappointing home defeat 2-1 to Gloucester City.

We saw off our promotion partner V.S Rugby comfortably by 4-1 and soon afterwards, local neighbours Corby Town were dismissed rather nonchalantly by 4-0 at the Rockingham Triangle – so it was not all bad news.

Whereas our FA Trophy hopes had ended so quickly the previous season, could this be our year?

Although Conference clubs had, and still do, dominate the Trophy, we nevertheless started to believe that we had a chance – be it that the early opposition had been rather moderate. Similarly the Dr Martens League KO Cup was also looking promising – how nice it would be to win the cup of the name of our patron saint! Wins against Rothwell Town, Bedworth United and Worcester City saw us progressing in the right direction.

We ended the old year with an away win 2-0 at Hastings Town and only two days later started the New Year equally well by winning 3-1 at home to Chelmsford Town in front of a new Nene Park record attendance of 2,523.

Two bad defeats followed, the first a somewhat surprising 2-0 setback at strugglers V.S Rugby and the second – where else but at Whaddon Road, Cheltenham and a spanking 3-0 into the bargain.

Would we ever get the better of them?

In the next five weeks, we were to achieve five victories where we scored 29 goals – an amazing goal glut with all three strikers, Nuttell, Watkins and Collins in terrific form saw defeats for Sittingbourne 5-0, Atherstone 7-1, Corby Town 6-1, Leek Town 5-0 and Halesowen 6-1 in the FA Trophy. Interspersed between these results were two 'doubles' of the wrong nature, losing to Gresley Rovers and Gloucester City yet again.

In the 4th Round of the FA Trophy, we were drawn away to Enfield and a Tim Wooding goal was just enough to secure a 1-1 result. Three days later at Nene Park in the replay, 3,007 fans (another increased record attendance) witnessed one of the great fight-back results.

Enfield had built up what looked like a sustainable 3-1 lead but when manager Roger Ashby switched Darren Collins from a wide left position to central striker, the game was transformed. He reduced the arrears and Adie Mann – a player who should have played all of his career in the Football League – equalised with only minutes remaining.

Collins, enjoying his new attacking role, dashed Enfield's hopes altogether in extra time by scoring again – a splendid 4-3 win with a two-legged semi-final against one of the finest

# FULL STEAM AHEAD

non-league cup teams in recent history, Woking, under the expert eye of manager Geoff Chapple, and wizardry of Chelsea player Clive Walker awaited us.

The Peter Debanke Terrace had now opened, midfielder Steve Spooner (now a full time coach at the club) had added guile to the centre of the pitch and we were sitting nicely in the league.

It couldn't get any better.

No, but it could get worse. And it did.

*Prince Charles arrives at Nene Park by helicopter.*

Firstly, we had thrown away a 2-goal advantage in the first leg of the semi-final of the Dr Martens League KO Cup by losing the return away leg 4-0 at Leek Town. Then we had blown any chance of league promotion with two awful consecutive defeats by Hednesford, 5-2 away, and eight days later by 3-2 at home. All of this, just when we wanted to hit form ready for Woking.

The first leg of the FA Trophy Semi-Final was at Nene Park on Saturday April 8th 1995.

It was particularly significant if for no other reason than on the Friday, the day before, Prince Charles officially opened the Diamond Centre. It is indeed a rare event for any of the

*Prince Charles with Mark Darnell.*

# Ten of Diamonds

senior royalty to open such a building, but as Max was patron to the Prince of Wales Trust, and Charles was due to visit us in this capacity, what better opportunity than to make a request which was subsequently granted.

He arrived by helicopter which landed in the centre circle of the pitch. There was no need for the normal 'H' to be painted on the ground, which is accorded such landings. I particularly recall joking with Prince Charles on this subject and saying that I hoped the pilot hadn't messed up our centre circle because we had a big match the next day! He assured me that he hadn't. He also wished me the best of luck, and I figured that we would need it.

Yet another ground attendance record and this time, 4,375, over a thousand improvement, saw us in sparkling form. However the final result was in no way a reflection of our superiority on the day. A 19th minute goal by Adie Mann had followed by Ian King (Max called him 'King of Diamonds'), hitting the inside of the post and the ball racing across the face of the goal to safety.

Dale Watkins was unfit for the game and Darren Collins together with Mickey Nuttell led the attack. I make particular reference to this because of subsequent events one week later.

We all felt that we had deserved at least a two goal lead to take to Woking, but we doubted that Clive Walker would again have such a quiet game – and he didn't.

Amazingly, Adie Mann, our most inventive player and scorer in the first leg, was left out of the starting line-up. The manager decided that he wanted Dale Watkins back with Mickey Nuttell and subsequently moved Darren Collins back to the wide left berth. It turned out to be a disastrous move. Darren played like a player totally disinterested, and this in a semi-final with Wembley being the next step.

It was unbelievable and Darren, whilst totally out of order for his apparent lack of effort, I still believed that Roger had brought this upon himself to some extent. If it's not broke, don't mend it, is the old adage.

Woking took a one goal lead in the opening half and so therefore we were all square but at half time, Adie Mann replaced Darren Collins amidst great speculation but Woking were well in control by this time.

Clive Walker had returned to his best form and when he scored midway through the second half it was Woking who would be going to Wembley to face Kidderminster Harriers. Our dream journey was over.

At a Board Meeting soon after the FA Trophy disappointment, manager Roger Ashby requested that Darren Collins be put on the transfer list. This followed the fracas surrounding the half time substitution of Collins and his performance at Woking.

Whilst normally the Board would always endeavour to back the manager, it was felt that there could be a major backlash from the fans if such a proposal was agreed.

Furthermore, there was always another day and Collins was a very important member of our club. To replace him would have been almost impossible at that time, so therefore we did not accede to Roger's request. Our decision was to be confirmed as the correct one, as Darren in the next three seasons went on to become one of the most prolific goalscorers in senior non-league football. He was to become the leading goalscorer in the club's history.

Fulfilling league fixtures with very little at stake, usually leads to some boring under-par matches. Particularly after a euphoric cup run with the Wembley mirage only a touch away.

Added to the FA Trophy eleven games (there were three replays) we played another eight Dr Martens League KO Cup encounters and three Northants Senior Cup matches, thank goodness we did get beaten in our one FA Cup tie at Eastwood Hanley,

Twenty three cup games in total can only lead to one thing – chaos!

From April 22nd to May 6th we played eight league matches, including four in five days; not altogether surprising that we only won two of them.

Hednesford were worthy champions with 93 points, seven clear of runners-up Cheltenham Town. We finished up in 5th place with 68 points, which considering it was our

## FULL STEAM AHEAD

first season in the league, plus our strenuous cup runs, this was not too bad. In the end, the players just ran out of steam and also just missed scoring the magical century of goals by one. Just to prove our goalscoring prowess, the champions Hednesford netted exactly the same total of 99. Even more surprising was that Burton Albion who finished in 3rd spot scored only 55 goals from the 42 games.

Dale Watkins, who missed 14 league games through injuries, was leading scorer with 25 goals (35 in all competitions) – virtually a goal every game. Darren Collins with 17 league (28 in total) goals, and Mickey Nuttell with 15 league (22 total) goals made it an impressive trio of strikers.

So what was the problem then? Why not a higher spot? 65 goals conceded tells the story, when both Cheltenham and Burton Albion both only had 39 goals against them.

A particularly pleasing statistic was the gate attendances. Our first season had a total of 17,000. The second season it had over doubled to 40,000 and now in year three it had leapt to a figure of 76,000. We were all delighted with this increase in support but it was Max who was smiling the widest – with an 'I told you so!' look on his face.

*Mickey Nuttell after scoring yet another goal.*

# 6
# THE JOY OF PROMOTION - AGAIN

**SINCE my retirement from my own business, I had been working on a 'free-gratis' part-time basis at Nene Park. In the early days I simply provided a guiding hand on any football administration matters as requested. I had always considered that it was a temporary arrangement and had no intention of retiring from one job and taking on another on a full-time basis.**

Subsequently, Mark Darnell, who had been a director and company secretary of the Griggs Group at Wollaston, had moved down to Nene Park and taken on responsibility of the Diamond Centre. He suggested to me that perhaps the time had come for a full-time Chief Executive to take on board both the Diamond Centre and the football club. The Diamond Centre was now in full swing with conferences, weddings and functions of any description – and yes, I could see this made sense.

So I went back to my gardening – only kidding – in reality it worked fine because Mark became Managing Director of the whole set-up, relinquishing his duties with Dr Martens factories while I said that I would continue to help out as and when required. I jokingly became the self-titled 'Minister without Portfolio' – do anything (well, almost!)

Meanwhile another major change in senior management job description occurred with Roger Ashby becoming a full-time manager. For three years he had performed his duties on a part-time basis, as was the case with all of the players. Like all managers in non-league football at that time, he had a normal day job and training was two nights a week.

The feeling was that if Roger gave up his job he would be able to provide the extra impetus and concentration needed for the push towards Conference football. I basically agreed with the thinking behind this suggestion but did not feel the timing was right, nor that Roger was the person for the job in the longer term. Now I realised that football management is not generally considered to be a job with long term prospects and I felt that in giving up his day job, Roger was leaving himself wide open.

If he failed and was relieved of his football position then I felt he could have difficulty in getting back a comparable job outside of soccer. When one is well into your forties, age becomes a stumbling block and companies are often loathed to recruit even the slightly older man.

Anyway, I didn't like the idea one little bit and said so to Max, who told me that he had already offered the job to Roger. It was the only time in ten years together that we had a real disagreement. Come to think of it, that's not a bad record!

My other concern was that eventually we would have full-time players and I just didn't think that Roger had the credentials or contacts that would undoubtedly be necessary. He had done a superb job at Irthlingborough Diamonds, then at Rushden Town and had achieved promotion with Rushden & Diamonds out of the Midland Division of the Southern League. Could he get another promotion? Well, he certainly proved me wrong on that one, but again,

## TEN OF DIAMONDS

it was at a given level and in the fullness of time my fears materialised on the higher plane.

So Roger became full-time manager in readiness for the new 1995-96 season with the rest of his staff and players remaining on a part-time basis. The obvious attention was focussed on the defensive frailties of the previous season. Out went centre half John Flower and left back Dave Johnson, both having served the club admirably. The two goalkeepers who had shared the majority of league matches. Kevin Fox and Martin Davies both left the club and Graham Benstead, an ex football league keeper with 200 such appearances behind him, joined from Kettering Town.

He was to be the first of several signings from our near neighbours Kettering Town over the ensuing months. Also from the Poppies was Roger's son Nick, a left back and natural replacement for Dave Johnson.

Ian King, Paul Richardson and Paul York were three more who departed from Nene Park in that summer. Centre half Al James Hannigan, who had impressed for Enfield against the Diamonds, and Glyn Creaser were the early choices as central defenders, but Creaser was probably a little past his best by this time and Steve Holden, also from Kettering Town, was to join and supersede him as the season unfolded.

*Andy Peaks*          *Brendon Hackett*

Andy Peaks who had been with the club from the outset, had just got better with each passing year and played the bulk of the games at the centre of defence. Gary Butterworth, who the previous season had played most games at centre half, was switched back to his preferred midfield position, playing all 42 league games. Although Steve Spooner was to be his partner for ten games, in the main it was another newcomer, Neil Smith, who linked up so determinedly in the middle of the park.

# The Joy of Promotion – Again

Brendan Hackett, a strong running outside left, was another new face at Nene Park and although right winger and crowd favourite Andy Kirkup had only been initially retained on a non-contract basis, he actually went on to play in 36 league matches, scoring eleven goals. He quickly dispelled any thoughts that releasing him would have been a good idea.

Probably the most contentious signing turned out to be Steve Lilwall from Kidderminster Harriers. Lilwall had made 73 appearances for West Bromwich Albion so we were obviously looking forward to seeing him play. As it turned out, he played only four league matches (nine in total) due to injuries and poor form. At no time did he ever look capable of having played at a much higher level.

However for me, the most surprising release of a player was Adie Mann. He could be difficult to handle and was a bit of a free spirit, but he had class – no doubt about that.

Earlier in the year, Kevin Keegan had been the main speaker at one of our celebrity sportsman's evenings in the Kimberley Suite. He spoke well, was in good form and promised Max that he would bring his first team squad to Nene Park for a pre-season friendly.

Easy to promise but another thing to deliver. Kevin Keegan did just that. He had just signed David Ginola and Les Ferdinand to add to his group of stars and sure enough much to our delight, they all descended upon Nene Park.

Our crowd capacity was limited to 4,600 at that time because of continuing ground improvements and we sold out immediately. One of the late stipulations from Kevin Keegan was that we allocated 50 seats for players wives, girlfriends and associates. As the game was a complete sell-out this was considered impossible to comply with but the message we received was do it – or else!

In consequence, we cleared the whole of the directors and officials seating area and Max and his wife Barbara together with myself and my wife Jean, sat on a balcony overlooking the corner of the pitch on stools! We were not entirely enamoured when the large seating area requested contained only four or five wives!

Having said that, we were delighted with the team that took the field against us although I don't think David Ginola on his debut was best pleased to be dumped on his backside by Al James. Newcastle won, as expected, by 3-1, with Dale Watkins scoring our goal.

The evening had been a huge success and certainly played in an excellent spirit which was more than could be said for the game played two days later.

The NFA Senior Cup against Kettering Town had been carried forward from the end of the previous season and a 2-2 draw hardly told the story of a fast, furious, no-holds-barred encounter. We were forced into another pre-season Cup replay only two days after the first one, and this time at Rockingham Road. We drew yet again at 2-2 only to lose the final in a penalty shoot-out.

After all this early season build-up, we just wanted to get down to the real business of winning the league and with it, promotion to the Conference.

Mickey Nuttell who had been such a prolific scorer in the past two seasons, was missing. Injuries eventually took such a toll on him that he started only one league match. Kevin Wilkin was Darren Collins new partner at the outset with our other scoring ace Dale Watkins on the bench. In fact Watkins was on the bench in 16 games and only started on 13 occasions in the league. Nonetheless he still scored 14 league goals – seemed strange, that!

We got off to the start that we needed with three opening consecutive league victories. The 2-1 away win at Chelmsford was memorable for two reasons – firstly Watkins coming off the bench netted the winner in the last minute and the other that I was introduced to England cricketer Ronnie Irani in the visitors boardroom.

Essex had been playing the West Indies on the adjacent ground – now open to supporters of both cricket and soccer – and as the cricket finished, the crowd simply moved over to watch our game, with some of the Essex players joining in for the tea and biscuits – or was it beer?!

An away defeat 4-2 at Burton Albion stopped us in our tracks but then followed a

# Ten of Diamonds

tremendous sequence of 13 league games of which we won 12 with one drawn. 6-1 against strugglers V. S Rugby who eventually finished bottom, 5-1 against Stafford Rangers and 7-3 against Atherstone United, all at Nene Park, were games to remember.

As we approached the Christmas period, another Kettering Town player joined us. Midfielder Steve Stott who was to play 17 league games in the second half of the season, was transferred for what I thought was an extortionate fee of £30,000. However at exactly the half way stage of 21 games played, we had a ten points lead over Cheltenham, our nearest rivals, so we were obviously on the right track.

In the FA Cup, we had progressed through to the first round proper and were rewarded with an attractive home tie against Cardiff City; this was to be the forerunner of good class football league opposition that we were to encounter in the FA Cup over the following years. We were beaten 3-1 by a much better team but never really did ourselves justice. Then again, we were never going to win the FA Cup!

Our other big hope in terms of Cup competitions was in the FA Trophy, particularly following our near miss the previous season. It turned out to be a disaster!

*Roger Ashby explains to his assistant Billy Jeffery how he sees things.*

Purfleet at Nene Park in the first round seemed a simple enough task. We had already beaten them in the FA Cup earlier that season, but lost horribly this time by 1-0.

So back to the league we went – after all, this was our holy grail – nothing else really mattered.

Apart from a surprising 3-2 home defeat by Gravesend and Northfleet we started to get our hopes back on track. Even so, the next seven games saw us win four times but three draws meant that six points had gone astray and it was Halesowen rather than Cheltenham Town that were creeping up on the rails. As it was, Cheltenham suffered a rare defeat at Nene Park by 4-1 – that felt good!

Halesowen away was a big match and by drawing 0-0 we figured that was nearly as good as a win, particularly as we were still comfortably in front. However another draw 1-1 at Ilkeston was a sure indication that winning this league was not going to be anywhere near as easy as many imagined.

Only a month earlier, Rushden & Diamonds had proudly led the league by 15 points, having played only one game more than Halesowen. By the time we were to play Halesowen at Nene Park at the end of March the lead was dwindling fast.

Action was called for and it came in the transfer of Carl Alford, yet another Poppies player for a fee that staggered the whole of the non-league football - £85,000! I thought that

# The Joy of Promotion – Again

was a crazy amount. This was a figure that was a record between non-league clubs and I thought it would stand for a very long time to come. Dover Athletic had previously paid £50,000 for David Leworthy from Farnborough Town, but this took it into another realm.

Carl Alford had been a major goalscorer at Kettering Town and it obviously had to be big money for the Poppies to agree to sell. As always, everything and everybody has a price; and Alford was to join us for the last ten matches to hopefully provide the extra icing on the cake – which in fairness he did by scoring on seven occasions.

But could he form a winning partnership with Darren Collins? The answer to that one would be provided in the following season because even from the outset, they looked an unlikely pair.

Anyway, he was signed in time for the Halesowen visit to Nene Park and it was generally considered that if we won this game, we were then very hot favourites for the title. A draw would be OK but a defeat was thinking the unthinkable, but that was how it turned out.

*Carl Alford*

Carl Alford netted on his debut but the visitor's centre half, a guy named Jim Rodwell, was magnificent in their deserved victory by 2-1. Now the fat really was in the fire. The league table said it all – although we still had two games in hand, our lead was down to three points!

The inconsistency continued with a 1-0 home defeat to Dorchester and we were now getting decidedly nervy. Although we managed a 2-1 home win against Cambridge City, two days later on Easter Monday we were thrashed 4-1 at Sudbury, although Alford scored with a fine diving header, his third goal in four games.

With six games still to play and the tension starting to show in the players' performances, we were now only two points clear with only one game in hand.

The one redeeming consolation in all this pressure was that we had a large goals difference advantage. Was it really going to come down to that?

Well maybe it was.

Another win for both clubs kept the status quo and then we had our 'catch-up' game at home to old rivals Gresley Rovers the following Tuesday. Collins and Alford scored in our 2-1 win, the winner from our new signing coming with only minutes remaining. Who said they couldn't play together?

We were now level matches with four games to play and five points in front. Surely we couldn't lose it now!

Gloucester City away was always going to be difficult as they were fourth in the league table and wanting their own back for a close defeat at Nene Park earlier on. It seems that we had achieved the minimum of a draw which would not have been too bad but agonisingly, an

# TEN OF DIAMONDS

injury time goal was conceded and we left Meadow Park with the knowledge that Halesowen had won at Gravesend.

This was really bad news and our lead was now just two points, level matches and three games still to play.

Of these three games, two were away and although we had beaten Salisbury and Stafford Rangers at Nene Park very easily – that was a long time ago.

Now it was pressure time.

I missed both matches as I had taken a week's holiday in Rome and Florence. This might seem strange with the championships in the balance but when I booked, we were fifteen points in front!

I remember ringing my daughter on the morning after the Wednesday night game at Salisbury from Rome to find out the result. Hallelujah – we won 2-0 thanks to goals from Collins and Kirkup.

Halesowen had not played in the week so our five point lead was restored but they still had a game in hand. Stafford Rangers were already relegated and apparently played like it. After only six minutes we were two goals up from Alford and Kirkup and two more later in the game saw us easy 4-0 winners.

*Andy Kirkup*

"How had Halesowen got on?", was the question everyone asked immediately as our game ended.

"Beat Baldock 1-0", was the disappointing reply.

There were only seven days of the season left. Halesowen were to travel to Crawley Town on the Tuesday evening and if they lost or drew, then Rushden & Diamonds were the champions. But they didn't lose or draw. Halesowen's incredible sequence of wins just continued, this time by 3-1, so we were back to level matches with our two point lead.

# The Joy of Promotion – Again

May 4th – the last match of the season – a season which had now turned into a cliff hanger.

Halesowen were away to Newport who were occupying a mid-table position and with very little to play for.

We were at Nene Park against Merthyr Tydfil, a team in 7th spot in the league, therefore no easy prey, although we had beaten them in Wales 3-0 at the end of October. We knew that a draw would be enough to win on goal difference. But could it really hinge on our 26- goal advantage?

By half time, the fans and particularly us directors, sipping our teas in the boardroom, all had big, big smiles on our faces – we led 3-0.

Alford, Butterworth and Collins had all scored – tension – what tension! We were surely home and dry. Nothing too sinister or miraculous could spoil our day. Could it? By scoring just before the interval, Darren Collins had netted his 30th league goal of the season (40 in total). Thank goodness we had not put him on the transfer list!

But wait; this game wasn't over yet.

Merthyr came out in the second half a different team. They swarmed all over us, got an early goal and threatened more but thankfully our defence held firm. With eight minutes remaining, Merthyr got a second goal and there was bound to be additional injury time – and there was. Please, please don't let us blow it now!

We were informed that Halesowen had won at Newport, and as the minutes ticked by, we were inching ever closer to the Conference. Max's dream and prophecy dating back to our first meeting at the ground before a brick had been laid on our stadium, was imminent.

The whistle signalled the end of the match and the end of the season. It was a tight 3-2 win but good enough to see us home by those two golden points.

Incredibly, Halesowen had finished 18 points ahead of third-placed Cheltenham Town, and when a team bags 92 points, it is invariably good enough to be the champions, but not that season.

*The Southern League, Premier Division Championship Trophy comes to Nene Park.*

# Ten of Diamonds

Also surprisingly, was that whereas we lost six league matches out of the 42 played, Halesowen lost only four! They were within touching distance of the Conference but as can so easily happen, their fortunes have since changed and have been a struggling club in recent seasons.

For the record, Garry Butterworth played in all 42 league matches (53 in total) and Darren Collins 41 (54 in total) – no better transfer money nor value for money had been spent by the club than on those two players.

The average league gate attendance had again increased from 1,521 to 2,166 and the individual match record had been broken again with a new figure of 4,664, which was the last game against Merthyr Tydfil.

We always have an end of season party at the club immediately after the last game and this one was very special. The Merthyr players and officials stayed on quite a while, joining us with our celebrations which I thought was rather nice. Even one of their officials apologised to me for putting us through the agony of those last few minutes.

Agony? "No problem", I said.

But the agony of the Conference was only three months away!

# 7
# SAVED BY B.T

**THE first major goal had been achieved - the Conference, or to give it its correct title, the GM Vauxhall Conference. The two promotions had taken four years but we were there now.**

We knew it was going to be very competitive but we had reached the pinnacle of non-league football and we were going to have to acclimatise very quickly. In retrospect, the season could be described in one sentence. It was initially exciting, becoming reflective then downright scary and ultimately thankful.

But we knew none of that at the beginning of the biggest adventure for the club so far. Two of our key forwards and main goalscorers Dale Watkins and Mickey Nuttell left the club.

Watkins, who joined Gloucester City, did so only after an administrative error allowed him to move on a free transfer. This was bad news because Dale, although an erratic performer and left out of the team a great deal the previous season, was nonetheless still young, quick and capable of scoring 15-20 goals in a season.

With Nuttell it was more understandable. He had been injured for a long period and there were obvious doubts as to whether he could perform well enough at the higher level. He subsequently joined Burton Albion, together with Steve Spooner. This did mean that Alford and Collins were earmarked for the two strikers spots with Kevin Wilkin as an alternative.

Kenny Cramman, a midfielder from Gateshead who reportedly had a penchant for goalscoring, was a major signing together with Mark Tucker who joined us from Woking where he had been particularly impressive against us in the semi-final of the FA Trophy.

However that was over a year earlier and I somehow doubt that he came with a clean bill of health. He was only 24 years of age but it was apparent very early on that he was struggling more like someone ten years older. He was to start in only six league games!

Before the season even started, Tucker was declared unfit and the same fate befell Steve Holden who also played only seven games the whole season. We quickly decided

*Jim Rodwell*

# Ten of Diamonds

that we needed an extra central defender to play alongside Al James Hannigan and Halesowen were contacted regarding Jim Rodwell who was still contracted to them. Halesowen didn't want to lose Rodwell who had been so intrumental in their bid for last season's championship. We all thought he would be an excellent signing and so it proved – not just that season, but the four following ones in the Conference. But Jim wasn't coming cheap!

Clubs were now very much aware that Rushden & Diamonds had, in their words, "a bottomless pit". This obviously wasn't the case but the signing of Carl Alford whilst still in the Southern League had signalled to all clubs, whether non-league or higher, that the club was prepared to pay big money for the right players.

Jim Rodwell cost the club £40,000 but we simply had to cover for two central defenders who were already on the treatment table before a ball had been kicked. The team which travelled to Altrincham was Benstead, Peaks, Ashby, Rodwell, Hannigan, Stott, Butterworth, Cramman, Wilkin, Alford, Collins and subs Hackett, Wooding and King.

It was interesting that Roger Ashby had opted for a 4-3-3 formation with Wilkin, Alford and Collins in attack. That selection was thrown into chaos when Alford was injured and had to be replaced by Brendan Hackett on the half hour.

Nonetheless the game was a cracking start to our baptism into the Conference. The lead changed hands four times and it seemed that the Diamonds were going to record a memorable 3-2 victory at a club which had enjoyed much success in the past. With only eight minutes remaining we were nearly there – what a start this promised to be!

Kenny Cramman had initially lived up to his reputation as a goalscorer by netting twice and the reliable Darren Collins had also opened his Conference account.

But it wasn't to be, as two dreadful defensive errors in the final minutes saw Altrincham snatch a victory which they never really deserved. Deserving and getting are two entirely different things – as we were to find out on more than this occasion.

The next game was a disaster, if that is the correct word to describe just losing a football match 5-0. Slough Town were rampant, Jim Rodwell was magnificent and keeper Graham Benstead decidedly shaky. Nine goals conceded in our opening two games was not what we had in mind.

Back at Nene Park for the next match – surely this would be OK. Not so. A Collins goal just salvaged a point against Northwich Victoria but another 1-1 draw at Hayes meant that we had just two points from a possible twelve. The 1-1 draw sequence continued for two more consecutive games. Firstly against Stalybridge Celtic at home – surely we could beat them – but we couldn't!

Then another home game, but this time it was Macclesfield who had been previous champions but had been refused promotion to the Football League on inferior ground status. The draw against the champions elect was OK and quite a good performance overall. However, four points from a possible eighteen meant we were in bottom place.

I recall this Macclesfield match very well for an entirely different reason. At half time, my two ex-business partners, Robert Langley, Chris Smith and myself continued sitting in the seats directly outside of the boardroom. We were in full view of the officials sipping their tea and biscuits and there was a degree of consternation as to what was going on.

I was told afterwards that Max said to Mark Darnell, "Are they going to resign or do you think they're plotting a takeover?" He was joking (I think).

In fact we were engrossed in negotiations for my final breakaway from our companies, Mayfayre/Abbey Vogue and this was a good opportunity with all three of us together.

\*           \*           \*           \*           \*           \*

The large new Airwair stand had been completed (minus a roof) in readiness of complying with possible promotion to the Football League and the need for a 6,500 capacity.

# Saved by B.T.

Somehow I didn't think we needed to worry too much on that scene! Survival might be more appropriate.

Whenever a club is in a state of flux, there is always player movement. Al James Hannigan was quickly on his way back to Enfield. Keeper Benstead was replaced by the signing of Martin Davies in his second spell at the club.

Terry Wilson who had found fame with Nottingham Forest but then suffered an horrendous knee injury, was drafted in, but he was another player that season to play only a handful of games. Then followed a win, in fact two wins and both were away from home. Halifax were beaten 3-1 and we got revenge at Northwich Victoria by 2-1, always a good place to win at!!

In both games, Jim Rodwell scored with headers, something he was to repeat on several occasions in the years to come.

Just as we thought that we had turned the corner, we embarked on a ten match run in which we recorded only one solitary win – a 3-0 home victory over ever-strugglers Welling United. Eight defeats in that awful spell, with only seven goals scored in those ten matches said it all – we were in big trouble!

Probably the worst was a 4-0 defeat by Gateshead at Nene Park. We had scored only 19 goals in our opening 18 league games of the season and particularly concerning was that both Collins and Alford had scored only twice each.

This Conference football was proving one hell of a lot harder that any of us could have believed. It was true that we had incurred a lot of injuries but the real crux was that we were simply not quite good enough – even to survive!

Then, as if to prove us doubters wrong, we won the next two games handsomely. Bath City were sunk comprehensively 4-1 at Nene Park and then we went one better with a 5-goal salvo away to Telford. Both Collins and Alford scored two each and Jim Rodwell obliged with another leader. Things were on the up?

It certainly didn't seem so in the next eight games. We went from bad to worse.

A 2-1 win at home against Morecambe was our only success and the six defeats and one draw surprisingly against championship challengers Kidderminster meant that we were rock bottom with only 25 points from 28 games! In an attempt to bolster our strike force Roger had made a good signing in David Leworthy from Dover Athletic. A proven goalscorer over many years and an ex-Tottenham Hotspur starlet, David was to prove invaluable, although his eight goals in eighteen games might not altogether suggest that.

Even our record in cup competitions was dismal. By playing against teams, all from lower leagues, we had progressed through to the first round in the FA Cup but then met Boreham Wood at Nene Park and lost 3-2. We had also gone out of the FA Trophy again at the first time of asking, beaten 2-1 at home to Farnborough Town. Even in the NFA Senior Cup we had no joy and a dreadful goalkeeping error by Martin Davies gave Kettering Town their winner in a 2-1 loss at Rockingham Road.

But it was our Conference position that was causing all the worry. It was Macclesfield at Moss Lane that I decided something drastic had to be done if we were to survive. By this time, Macclesfield had overturned a big Kidderminster lead and had taken over at the top of the league. We hardly could expect to win there and we didn't. A 2-1 defeat normally would be acceptable but not when the club is desperate for points.

In their boardroom after the match I took Max to one side and urged him to appoint an experienced coach to help Roger. I considered that more drastic action was needed than that, but I knew the chairman's loyalty to Roger meant that he would not consider replacing him. So that was my compromise suggestion.

I clearly remember saying, "Max, we saw today one team that is going up and one that is going down"

Relegation was staring us in the face.

# Ten of Diamonds

It was both mine and other director's opinions that Roger had taken the club as far as he possibly could. He had done a splendid job in achieving two promotions but this had been done at a lower level and with the chairman's considerable financial backing. He knew the lower non-leagues extremely well and had been able to get the best players. But now were in danger of relegation at the first time of asking.

Whilst I felt that it was time for a change in manager, I also knew that the chairman would not agree to this. He was too loyal. However I convinced him to advise Roger that we wanted to advertise for an experienced coach in a national newspaper, and this we did immediately.

A wide range of applications were received, with all sorts and sizes.

On the Friday morning before the home game against Slough Town (how well we recalled the early season 5-0 thrashing), Max appeared at my door. He had collected various CV's together and asked me to have a look through them. Then I remember saying, "Oh, I've got another one for you to add to this list – it's from Brian Talbot. He gave it to me on Wednesday night".

I had forgotten all about it.

What had happened was that on the previous Wednesday evening, Brian who had been working for the PFA, having recently returned from a 4-year stint in Malta, called to see me at home around teatime.

In the course of conversation, the team's current plight was discussed and Brian asked when the next game was. I told him, "On Saturday at home to Slough Town but we do have a reserve game at home tonight"

"In that case I'll come down to the game with you tonight", said Brian.

On arrival in the boardroom, Brian immediately saw Roger and started discussing the club's dilemma. It was then mentioned that we had just advertised for a coach and when Brian did not join me for the second half, I knew he must be in deep conversation with Roger. I also knew that Roger was wary of Brian because of his long relationship with me, which went back to our 1978 meeting when Bobby Robson first brought him to our club.

Later that evening, we sat in his car in the car park and he scribbled out a brief letter of application saying that he had just heard about the job advert and apologising for the limited content. I put the letter in my pocket and forgot about it!

In any case, I was just going through the motions because I knew Roger would not want Brian but nevertheless I gave the note to Max. In the afternoon, I went for a game of golf and thought nothing more about my conversation that morning with Max.

However Max decided to call a board meeting for the Friday afternoon. All the other directors were contacted and agreed to be present – all except me as I was somewhere on the fairway, or more likely in a bunker and not contactable.

When I returned from golf at around 5 o'clock, my daughter Alison who happened to be at my home at the time told me of a couple of phone calls advising me of the hastily arranged meeting. Would I go to the meeting on my return was the request. I rushed to the club, still attired in my golf kit, and burst into the boardroom where sitting there were the other six directors plus Roger Ashby.

Everyone was smiling – I'm not sure what they had to smile about, but I was informed by Max that I was too late and that a decision had been reached and provided that he would accept, Brian Talbot had been appointed as coach.

I was flabbergasted. Not because I didn't think he was the best man for the job, because I did. It was that Roger had accepted him without presumably too much of a struggle.

I said to Roger, "Are you happy about it because he is a strong character". "No problem", he replied. "Ok – but don't say I didn't tell you!" I added. Robert Langley also said that he had basically said the same thing earlier.

Anyway it was decided that Max would ring Brian that evening to offer him the job and invite him to the game against Slough Town the next day.

# SAVED BY B.T.

Job done.

Match day arrives and so does Brian. He sits in the stand just watching and observing while Roger and Billy Jeffrey, his assistant, were in their normal dugout roles. Suddenly in the second half with the game on a knife edge, BT makes his move. Everyone in the stand close by was wondering what was going on. I knew exactly!

He completely took over in the dugout, demonstrating to the players of his requirements while Roger and Billy looked on in rather dazed amazement. What I said would happen was happening but I never envisaged it so quickly or in this manner. Julian Capone, an exciting young player who was never able to fulfil his potential scored twice but the game ended 2-2. Another point, yes, but we were still bottom of the conference.

On the Sunday evening about 9 o'clock, my phone rang – it was Max.

He said, "Roger has just phoned me and he feels that he won't be able to work with Brian, and what with all the recent pressure, it would be best if he resigns". I was temporarily stunned. I knew there would be a problem but not of this magnitude within 48 hours. Max then added, "I think we should ask Brian to take over – what do you think?" I just said, "OK".

And that is exactly how it all happened.

\*       \*       \*       \*       \*       \*

Although Roger had resigned as Team Manager, he didn't want to leave the club and it was agreed that he should head up the Youth section.

It was not an entirely satisfactory solution as it meant that whilst they would not exactly be working together, there would be fairly regular contact and this was never going to be easy for Roger, seeing that he had been a successful manager for four years and now suddenly was beholden to Brian.

As it happened, an agreement was reached and Roger left Nene Park in January 1999. I think he felt that I was instrumental in all the goings-on and whilst it was true that I thought we required a new manager to save us from relegation, I was not at this board meeting, whereas he was and he should have voiced his misgivings at the time.

As it was I thought we had left it too late to get out of trouble. It would have been disastrous for Max, having spent so much money on the stadium and on players to see his dream of reaching the Conference disappear in our very first season.

However we dressed it up, we were bottom and six points behind the team in 19th place which was the spot we had to aim for. Simple as that!

*Brian Talbot follows Roger Ashby from the dug-out v. Slough Town.*

63

# TEN OF DIAMONDS

*David Leworthy celebrates his goal at Rockingham Road.*

Put another way, Brian had 13 games left to perform the miracle that might just be needed. By an incredible coincidence his very first game was against Kettering Town at Rockingham Road. The Poppies were on an eight match unbeaten turn and had won the previous five home games.

They would certainly be ready for Mr Talbot who they had not forgotten from his unhappy alliance with the club and its short term owner, a certain Mark English. That whole episode had gone 'pear-shaped' very quickly. English had virtually disappeared and Brian was left to sort out the financial mess. It was a very unhappy time for Brian and although he was the innocent front man for Mark English, it nevertheless left a nasty taste at Rockingham Road.

So here he was back there attempting to save the Poppies old enemy from relegation. I was there that day at Rockingham Road and can assure you that is was no place for the faint hearted. 4,600 fans were there also and most baying for blood, but it didn't work out that way.

Never could a game have gone so well for a new manager in a hostile environment and with so much depending on the result. A spectacular 5-1 win for the Diamonds sent the Poppies fans home despondent. David Leworthy was irrepressible with two fine goals and ex-Poppy Alford, Hackett and Butterworth scored the others. Could this be a turning point? Yes it could and yes it was!

Five consecutive wins means fifteen points and we were climbing from the bottom basement – fast. Bromsgrove Rovers and Kettering Town again were both very tight 1-0 wins but as they say – a win is a win.

Telford at home 2-0 and Welling away 1-0 again completed Brian's opening five games. Two draws against Dover and Hayes kept us picking up the points. Bath City away were next on the list and they were fighting relegation themselves. A fight they eventually lost but on that particular day they won 3-2 in a tremendous fight back which saw David Mehew (soon to become a Diamond) get the winner deep in injury time.

Carl Arlford was now getting regularly on the score sheet with four goals in three matches but the one he scored at Stevenage Borough was only a consolation in a bad 4-1 mauling. Stevenage certainly showed why they were third in the league that evening and a certain Michael Mison, on loan from Fulham, scored a super goal. Mison was to join the Diamonds in the summer as one of Brian Talbot's new signings.

One other interesting appearance for the Diamonds during those hectic final matches was goalkeeper Steve Cherry. Interesting in so much that Cherry had been on loan to

# SAVED BY B.T.

Kettering Town and played against the Diamonds in their 1-0 defeat. The following week he was signed for the rest of the season by the Diamonds and played against Telford again at Nene Park.

Three games to go and although we had suffered two bad defeats we knew that a home win against Halifax would certainly guarantee survival and almost send our opponents out of the league. A cruel game, this football.

A Brendan Hackett goal was enough to clinch all three points and Halifax looked doomed. Amazingly they survived with a win and a draw against top opposition while Bath City missed out by one point and went down.

Onto the very last league game of the season and it finished how it started, against Altrincham. They had been in free-fall throughout the second half of the season and were already certain of relegation when they arrived at Nene Park. The game ended 3-2 in Diamonds favour, but it was Garry Butterworth who made the headlines for three reasons. He had received the Player of the Year award before the game, scored a rare goal and with a header – then got unceremoniously sent off for a bout of fisticuffs. A good day, Garry!

Rushden & Diamonds finished in 12th spot, a truly remarkable feat considering their dire circumstances two months earlier.

Macclesfield were promoted having beaten Kidderminster Harriers by five points to the championship.

Who cared? We certainly didn't. We had won our own personal championship – 8 wins, 3 draws and 2 defeats in the 13 matches under Brian was a remarkable way to finish this season.

The attendance record had gone yet again with the 5,170 against neighbours Kettering Town. BT had certainly given everyone at Nene Park something to smile about, but could he repeat his success with a completely fresh start in a new season?

All would be revealed.

*Garry Butterworth in action.*

# 8
# CONFERENCE CONSOLIDATION

**IN the summer of '97, Brian Talbot had many things on his mind.**

He knew that last season's survival, though absolutely vital, could now only be considered as a stepping stone for Conference consolidation, or hopefully a little more.

Whilst contracts were up for some of the players he inherited, and some would therefore leave, there were others that he encouraged to find new clubs earlier than they expected.

He figured that a wholesale clearout was unfortunately necessary, but that this would mean a lot of hard work in finding replacements – in a league and level which he knew precious little about.

Quite apart from mostly playing at the top level, he had also spent four years out of the country. In the two months with the Diamonds, he had obviously observed opposition players, and watched numerous games at the end of that season in the hope of finding a gem.

His diligence was not unrewarded when he discovered a player who was at Enfield but had only ever played in London non-league circles. That player was Paul Underwood, and he was a gem. Although he was to start in only 25 of our 42 league games that coming season and have the fans somewhat divided as to his capabilities, he was eventually to become, in Brian's opinion, his best ever signing and a player of the highest calibre.

In the fullness of time he would also become club captain and someone that the other players and the fans regard as 'numero uno'. Although he is now considered the complete

*Paul Underwood*

# Ten of Diamonds

left full back, he did in those early days at the club play wide left in front of Kenny Cramman, who had been converted from midfield to the full back role by BT.

However Paul Underwood was still under contract at Enfield and they, like all the other clubs, were aware of the money which Max Griggs had spent so far. They demanded a fee of £60,000 which was much too high. Something in the region of one third of that figure – maybe up to £25,000 at a push, because Paul was an untried player even at Conference level.

Brian was so certain about him that the asking fee was met. I was uncertain about the size of the amount to be paid, but Max was on a roll and Brian got his man.

*John Hamsher and Michael Mison.*

Michael Mison, a strong 6 foot 3 midfielder who we had all seen at Stevenage was a free agent and joined us. He promised so much and Brian stuck with him for perhaps longer than he should. He did have real potential but that is all it ever was.

Another Fulham lad, John Hamsher, just appeared with Mison and asked for a trial and stayed three years. He was a lovely lad, incredibly fit and the best penalty taker I think I've ever seen. Three years on, John just wasn't quite of the standard BT required and he then moved on.

Danny O'Shea was available on a free transfer and had been assistant to Ian Atkins, manager of the Cobblers and earlier in his career had played a few games for Arsenal when BT was at Highbury. He had still been a regular player at Northampton Town the previous season but was unfit from the start. He only ever started one league game and didn't finish that. He seemed a very likeable man but it was one signing that was doomed from the start.

# Conference Consolidation

In wanting to add another striker to his squad, BT went back for an old West Bromwich Albion days player when Adrian Foster (Fozzy) was there with him as a youngster. In more recent times, he had been with Hereford United and was transferred from them also that summer. However Fozzy was another player to start the season injured and during the whole of the season only made 14 starts in league games.

But it was the exodus of players from Nene Park that showed BT's real intent. Ten players were to leave in all and that was all in the summer – others followed later.

Nuneaton Borough bound were three forwards of varying types – Richard Bailey who had promised so much but just didn't progress, Ian King and Kevin Wilkin who had fought injuries all his career but had still scored 43 goals from 95 total games and with only 66 starts. Quite a remarkable record but he always was considered fragile.

Goalkeeper Graham Benstead had been questionable on several occasions

*Chris Whyte and Adrian Foster.*

and had lost his place at the back end of the season to Steve Cherry – he joined Kingstonian, an old London club who were showing their intent with some high profile signings.

None more so than David Leworthy who had only joined the Diamonds in the latter stages of last season. The problem with David was that he lived on the South coast and travelling from this distance soon palled. This was never going to continue for very long, but he was there for us when we needed him. In selling Leworthy to Kingstonian, we received £5,500 more than we paid to Dover Athletic.

Nick Ashby was expectedly released and joined Burton Albion, Steve Lilwall went back to from whence he came (Kidderminster Harriers) and Steve Holden was sold to Stevenage Borough for a nominal amount.

To complete BT's cull, Neil Smith who had captained the promotion winning side joined Hednesford and the injury prone Mark Tucker limped off to join the Poppies at Rockingham Road.

In addition to the playing staff, there was also a new appointment in BT's 'in-house' team. So when Simon Parsell became the club physiotherapist, he not only offered the players the benefit of his healing skills, but also became the team humorist and 'agony aunt'. A regular contributor to the matchday programme, he is now a sparkling wit on the club's own 'Radio Diamonds'.

On the medical side of the business, he has formed a unique pairing with the one and only, irrepressible Dr Mark Pepperman, known affectionately to everyone at the club as 'Doc'.

Brian had also discussed with the chairman his desire to turn the club into a full-time outfit as soon as possible. For this season, there would have to be a split with some full-time and other existing contracted players who were part-time. It was not ideal but would only be for one season – or that was the intention.

# Ten of Diamonds

*L-r: Simon Parsell, Dr Mark Pepperman and Terry Westley hard at work.*

However after a poor start – in fact an awful start – which showed only one point from the opening four games – further action was necessary.

Three straight defeats came against Northwich Victoria at home, and Farnborough Town and Leek Town, both away without scoring a goal before achieving our first draw, a 1-1 scoreline with Hednesford Town.

Two wins followed against Gateshead 3-2 at home and Slough Town 2-1 away before meeting up with our old Southern League rivals Cheltenham Town at Whaddon Road. Cheltenham had been promoted to the Conference having finished runners-up to Gresley Rovers but the latter's ground didn't meet the necessary criteria so up came Cheltenham.

Our ex-striker Dale Watkins had joined them via Gloucester City and certainly rubbed salt in our open wounds by scoring the second in a 2-0 emphatic win.

*Darren Bradshaw*

70

# Conference Consolidation

With BT starting to put pressure on players now to go over to full-time, Steve Stott and Andy Peaks were soon casualties. Both had good jobs outside of football and were understandably not prepared to commit. The changeover of players was gathering pace and soon it was to be goodbye to keeper Steve Cherry and welcome to his replacement Mark Smith. But the two signings which started to really turn things around were centre half Chris Whyte of Arsenal and Leeds United fame and Darren Bradshaw who had travelled and played at clubs the length and breadth of the country.

Although Darren Bradshaw played his first couple of games somewhat unimpressively in midfield, he soon settled down with Chris Whyte to form a splendid central defender partnership. Both players immediately became firm favourites of the fans.

A free transfer was Mark Smith, who had played at Crewe Alexandra and Walsall and was undoubtedly our best keeper so far – he had a somewhat chequered background but was a smiling face around the club. He could be a little erratic to say the least, but was similarly spectacular.

*Colin West asks "What's the problem, ref?"*

## Ten of Diamonds

Another interesting new face that belonged to an 18 year old who looked 10 years older was tough guy Guy Branston. He came on loan from Leicester City and stayed for ten league games.

While all of this was going on – believe it or not – we actually played some football matches. We beat Kidderminster Harriers twice in the space of a month, 2-1 away and 4-1 at home.

Another short-term loan player was Justin Barnwell-Edinboro who played only 4 games but scored 3 goals, all in one game against Kidderminster.

There was no doubt that the sweeping changes in personnel that BT had carried out were having the desired effect. We were creeping up the league nicely, be it that we were still 10 points adrift of who other than Halifax, the team that escaped relegation from the Conference only a few months earlier by the skin of their teeth.

In the NFA Senior Cup, which unfortunately these days is in terminal decline, sent us to Brackley Town who were two leagues below us in status.

There were three quite separate reasons which made this tie worth remembering. Firstly, it was played throughout pouring rain on an absolute sea of mud; secondly Darren Collins scored a splendid hat trick and could have had six; but most of all for the appearance in midfield of 43 year old manager Brian Talbot.

I have no idea what made Brian turn out, other than I can only assume that he just wanted to play another full game of football!

Well he finished the evening off by being taken to Kettering General Hospital feeling decidedly poorly, and I recall picking him up from there at around 2 o'clock in the morning and taking him to my home. As far as I am aware, he didn't ever do it again!

After we had beaten Kettering Town 1-0 at Nene Park in a very tight encounter, we spoiled our progress badly by losing 3-1 at home to Hayes. We then finished the old year off very nicely with four consecutive wins.

Another new face at Nene Park was Colin West, an old Watford team mate of BT who was drafted in to the side to give Darren Collins the supply power which was to provide him with his best goalscoring record to date.

It also coincided with BT becoming increasingly disdainful over Carl Arlford's contribution who only started four league games that season.

It was just as well that Christmas had come with our league position far healthier because our form in Cup competitions was far from impressive. In the FA Cup we had been beaten in a 4th Qualifying round replay at home 1-0 by Boreham Wood, and we had lost 2-0 at Hayes in the league KO Cup.

In the month of January our depressing Cup form continued with a 1-0 home defeat to Raunds Town in the NFA Senior Cup and only four days later departed from the FA Trophy second round losing 3-1 again at Cheltenham courtesy of two fine goals by Dale Watkins yet again.

Mark Cooper, son of the famous Terry Cooper of Leeds United repute, also joined us. It was one big merry-go-round. After beating Southport at home 1-0 and Dover Athletic away 3-0 we then had the BIG ONE – Halifax Town at Nene Park.

They were still well clear at the top of the table and a young striker named Geoff Horsfield was scoring every match – well almost.

Horsfield who a year later joined Fulham and only last season scored in the Football League Division 1 play off final which took his latest club Birmingham City into the Premiership, was on that particular day – anonymous!

It was Darren Collins who looked the Conference's brightest scoring star as they battled for recognition for the Golden Boot award. The scoreline of 4-0 in our favour shook the league to the core. Halifax had succumbed to the best display by the Rushden Diamonds hitherto seen at Nene Park.

# Conference Consolidation

The Halifax lead had been cut down to 8 points and with 15 matches still to play – who knows?

After the Lord Mayor's Show we were sent packing 2-1 in a dreadful display due to defensive errors and missed chances galore against Gateshead up on Tyneside. In my own mind, that was the end of any possible challenge to Halifax. We were simply too inconsistent. This was borne out the following weekend when we went back into the lion's den at Rockingham Road and thrashed the Poppies 4-0.

A 3-0 win at Nene Park against Stalybridge Celtic was followed by a heart-warming win by 4-1 at home to Cheltenham Town. A 2-0 win away to Woking meant 12 points, a maximum haul, had been collected since the Gateshead debacle. BT had moved into the market yet again by signing Farnborough Town's David Mehew who had a proven goalscoring pedigree in both the Football League and non-league soccer.

Halifax's 0-0 scoreline at Hednesford gave the Diamonds once again a sniff of the title and with a visit to The Shay imminent, we had moved convincingly into second spot, ten points adrift but with a game in hand.

A win at Halifax was essential to put them under real pressure but it never looked likely to happen. Darren Collins was suspended and that was a major blow. He was playing the best football of his career and Halifax remembered only too well his power and pace from their last meeting at Nene Park. This time they were never troubled and a 2-0 defeat let the Diamonds off lightly.

Hednesford away two days later was not a place for despondent footballers but yet again illustrating our topsy-turvy form, the Diamonds snatched a 1-0 win with a tremendous effort from young Hamsher.

The Morecambe game I remember so well because if anyone thinks that a game is dead and buried when a team leads 3-0, then think again.

That was the half time scoreline at Nene Park after a display which ranked alongside the dismantling of Halifax six weeks earlier.

How many more could we score in the second 45 minutes? Answer – none, but Morecambe could and did, by netting three times to draw level, and could easily have won it. Again the frailties were exposed in a poor performance the following week, losing 4-2 at Telford. The back wheels had already come off and we were in danger of losing the front ones as well.

We sure enough did just that when in the final five games we lost twice at home to Leek Town and Welling United both by the same scoreline of 1-0 – we were awful!

The final home game had to be won to ensure that we finished 4th and keep Morecambe from overtaking us. This we managed with a 3-2 win over Telford United, with Collins scoring two more. He was even given the opportunity to score from the penalty spot (which he did) in an effort to oust Geoff Horsfield as the Conference leading goalscorer but his 29 league goals was not quite enough. In total, he netted 35 goals that season. No one else got into double figures, even taking all competitions into account!

Telford, Gateshead and Stalybridge were the bottom three but Telford remarkably were reprieved and Slough Town who finished in 8th position were tossed out of the league for the inability to be represented at the Conference AGM and the uncertainty that surrounded their chances of continuing in business.

Halifax were worthy champions winning by a clear 9 points from Cheltenham Town who had finished so strongly in their very first season in the Conference.

Woking were third on the same number of points (74) as Rushden and Diamonds but had a four-goal difference advantage to their credit. After the dreadful start I suppose 4th spot could be considered a good achievement but it had been a season that promised so much at different times. In ringing so many changes of personnel which Brian thought was necessary – and I entirely agreed – it meant that at no time was there a settled formation.

# Ten of Diamonds

33 different players had started games in the League programme – a colossal amount. The total gate attendance was virtually identical to the previous season which was a little surprising considering the team were at one stage challenging for promotion compared with fighting for survival a year ago.

The building work, comprising of a new office block, four new hospitality suites and the large new Executive Lounge and the 'Doc Shop' had all been completed behind the North Stand.

The playing staff for next season would be exclusively full-time, and Cyril Lea who many years ago was assistant to manager Bobby Robson at Ipswich when BT was a young lad, would now be joining the coaching and scouting staff.

Everything pointed to an interesting next season – would it be the third time lucky for the Rushden & Diamonds?

*Cyril Lea, Chief Scout.*

# 9
# HOSPITALITY, CELEBRITIES AND THE EMERALD ISLE

**WEST HAM UNITED have been sponsored by the Griggs Group for a few years now and the splendid new stand at Upton Park bears the name of Dr Martens.**

In consequence West Ham have played pre-season friendlies at Nene Park as a partial 'thank you' and in the summer of 1998 there was an additional reason for their presence.

The official opening of the Doc Shop.

Manager Harry Redknapp and player Paulo di Canio did the honours and together with a couple of our players, were signing autographs and being photographed by fans who flocked into our new emporium. Every conceivable souvenir imaginable relating to the club, together with replica kits of all dimensions and variations, are on sale there.

However there is also a vast range of Dr Martens footwear on display, hence the name – the Doc Shop.

Taking pride of place as senior saleswoman in the shop is Audrey Lake, who has not only been with the club since its conception ten years ago, but who prior to that was a Rushden Town stalwart at Hayden Road alongside her club secretary husband Bernard, for many years.

The Doc Shop was part of a large extension to the North Stand, which was deemed necessary to accommodate more people, both in office accommodation and hospitality. The attractive entrance to the Rushden & Diamonds Football Club's main reception – not to be confused with its salubrious sister at the Diamond Centre at the other corner of the stadium – leads upwards to a suite of eight offices.

Stopping off halfway up the stairs, one will immediately see the 'roll of honour' boards proudly displayed as a reminder of the players awarded the yearly accolades.

We needed another sizeable function suite similar to the Kimberley in the South Stand in order to cater for our patrons who are the companies who pay for the privilege on match days of wining and dining in lovely surroundings directly overlooking the pitch.

This we named the Executive Lounge. Apart from its use on match days the other main thinking was for it to be used on weekdays for other functions and seminars.

That summer the official opening of the new Executive Lounge and the hospitality suites was carried out in a poignant ceremony in which both my wife and I were particularly involved, as were other relatives of the people after whom the suites are named.

I had the honour of making the appropriate speech in front of an audience of carefully selected guests, all of whom had past connections with the original clubs. It had been decided that the four chosen figures who gave so much as the founding fathers of Rushden Town and Irthlingborough Diamonds be remembered and honoured in this way.

One suite was to be retained with a specific purpose for the Griggs company's desired needs for entertaining, and was named the Dr Martens Suite. However the other suites were

# Ten of Diamonds

*David Knighton*

named after David Knighton, Cyril Jones, Ken Ambridge and Cyril Freeman. It is so pleasing to hear a girl receptionist talking to a client by saying, "You will be in the David Knighton suite, Sir". She may not know who David was and it's very likely that the customer doesn't know either, but the club knows and in their names being regularly voiced in this manner, it ensures that they will always be remembered.

I will now endeavour to tell you why those people were all considered worthy of their names becoming synonymous with the Rushden & Diamonds Football Club.

So who was David Knighton?

To the old die-hard supporters of Irthlingborough Diamonds and opposing clubs, together with many local townsfolk, David's name, antics and flamboyant reputation was a byword.

He was an Irthlingborough boy, educated at Wellingborough Grammar School and being a big lad, was initially a rugger type. Although he played rugby at the school, he nevertheless played soccer for the Diamonds Under 18 side and was a rather forgettable centre forward.

Could he play?

No, not really, but he would always remind everyone who would listen of the time he scored twice in the NFA Youth Cup, beating the hitherto unbeatable Cobblers Youth 4-3 in the final. It was his greatest day as a player.

Much more significantly, David who was known to almost everyone as 'Bruiser' at 17 years of age joined the Diamonds Committee. It was a sure sign that he had called it a day as a player – see what I mean when I called him a forgettable centre forward!

In doing so, he emerged as a character that would always be synonymous with the old Diamonds club. We became very close friends and worked together on numerous projects and in particular on turning a barren field into the first Nene Park.

In his thirties and forties, he always wore a deerstalker. On anyone else it would have looked ridiculous but this was 'Bruiser'. He was an eccentric; he knew it and played up to it. Over the years and during a time when the Diamonds were so successful, he helped make it so.

He was our clubhouse supremo; he was our master fundraiser and simply an extrovert extraordinaire. I used to call him that. I think he rather liked it.

The strange thing in our relationship was that we argued a lot, although David always called it "debating"! At a time when our average gates were around 300, David's fundraising expertise and enthusiasm was legendary.

He organised 'The Long Game' which comprised of a five-a-side football competition where players swapped regularly but nonetheless played for 24 hours non-stop on an indoor pitch inside the Express Hall of John Shortlands Footwear. The idea was for someone to predict the correct (or nearest) score. I seem to remember that over 800 goals were scored but

# Hospitality, Celebrities and the Emerald Isle

much more importantly, we raised over £1,000 which today would be worth ten-fold.

He also organised 'The Big Walk', over a 20 mile course with over 100 walkers taking part. It was a forerunner of such events locally and again topped the thousand quid mark. Another original idea of his was called 'What's D Time?' A watch was hidden away in the local Co-Op store safe and the participants had to fill in a form guessing the correct time at which the watch stopped.

Yet another huge moneymaker!

Barbecues at farmer Jack Brown's Addington farmyard were another big yearly event. Dances with a big band sound, cabaret evenings – all organised by David.

Oh, and for good measure, he organised the weekly tote!

The large picture in the suite of his name shows him in a bowler hat as barman at a Grand Western night. Peter De Banke arrived at the clubhouse in a large stetson and riding a real live stallion. Those were the days! I don't think those days can ever be repeated again.

He had been on the committee for 31 years, it just doesn't seem possible – when he passed away at the early age of 48. David was simply a one-off.

I know he would have fought me tooth and nail over the merger with Rushden Town, but he would have come round. He always did. He would have been a massive asset to our club today but we can only thank him for what he did in those early days and for his presence in our lives.

I think and talk of him so very often, and he will always now be remembered in his own special suite.

*My father, Cyril Jones.*

# Ten of Diamonds

The Cyril Jones suite is a memorial to my father. He was the chairman of the Irthlingborough Diamonds and took on this mantle in 1947 when we started the club. The fact of being chairman as such didn't really mean that much because we were only a small local club but he did so very much in so many other ways.

Even so he never missed a Monday evening committee meeting which in the early days was held at the 'Sow and Pigs' inn (now renamed the Oliver Twist) and then later 100 yards down the road to The Horseshoe. I can't remember quite why we moved but I guess it was to do with their genial landlord Jack Garley. Subsequently we moved our headquarters to Nene Park but before the original boardroom was built, we simply had our Monday meetings in the home team dressing room.

Father was the quiet dignified man at the head of the Irthlingborough Diamonds in those days. I certainly cannot claim to have acquired too many of his genes or gentle attributes. Whenever I was chasing around at a hundred miles an hour, father was the steadying hand on the tiller. He had a knack of saying the right thing at the right time.

He was a 'hands-on' man and could do more or less everything that a small football club needed. In those early days he would select and blow up the best five balls we had. Not very demanding one might think but lacing up a ball was an art form in itself. A badly protruding lace section could cut open a forehead so very easily. He would heavily dubbin these large brown balls – nothing so classy as white or orange ones – and then decide carefully which was to be the match ball!

He would then proceed to the Recreation ground, crawl under the bandstand where the posts/crossbars and nets were all stored. Then with a little help from son, he would erect the goalposts and fix the nets. Then he would mark the pitch out. Nothing special but it all had to be done – every home game, year after year.

It was a council owned ground but we had no groundsman assistance. But when you don't know any different, it's no big deal. Even in the early days at Nene Park, father would continue with the same jobs until he felt that he was a bit too old. I don't know what he would have said about the splendid stadium pitch of today. Probably, "If I had had that much equipment I could have done the same!"

Fortunately my father did see the first three years of the new stadium's construction and watched many matches from his seat inside the boardroom in the warmth, alongside Robert Langley's and Chris Smith's dads. Talk about 'Last of the Summer Wine'.

I thought of him when we went to Cardiff's wonderful Millennium Stadium – he would never have believed that the club would ever have reached such an elevated milestone.

Incidentally there is a fine oil painting of my father in the suite of his name. I would think he was in his mid-sixties at the time it was painted by Jeremy Barlow who I knew very well and has since gone on to make quite a name for himself painting landscapes in East Anglia. Anyway, the 40 years which father gave to the old Irthlingborough Diamonds was rewarded by the suite of his name. Rather nice, I thought.

\*        \*        \*        \*        \*        \*

The Ken Ambridge and Cyril Freeman suite is a 'double header'. It is a larger suite which is devoted to these gentlemen who for a combined 76 years, guided and were committed to the cause of Rushden Town and its ground at Hayden Road.

Cyril Freeman was the first of these two long-serving secretaries, so let's talk about him.

For starters, there would be very few of our fans today who would ever have heard of him because he died over fifty years ago. Cyril Freeman was literally Mister Rushden Town. He was widely regarded as the architect of the Russians continued success in the pre-war years.

Although obviously the manager and particularly the players were directly instrumental in winning matches and thereby championships, it was Cyril who pulled all the strings. He

# HOSPITALITY, CELEBRITIES AND THE EMERALD ISLE

*Cyril Freeman*

was club secretary but in name only. He did everything! His reign lasted 30 years from 1919-1949, during which time he chased and signed players and made the Hayden Road ground a fortress. His wife washed the kit and did all the things that wives of dedicated football men have always done – gave the utmost support.

The NFA Senior Cup was regularly ensnared by the Russians in those heady days. Twelve times they were winners.

The Cobblers and Poppies were their main adversaries and always over 5,000 fans would be crammed into the ground for those matches. Apparently trophies were stored under the bed at the Freeman household. Being a formidable and evocative Northants Football Association Councillor, he felt it his duty to his club and his county to house such expensive and important silverware in the safest possible place! It is said that Cyril had access to all the best Northamptonshire players by virtue of his County FA sources. I'm not sure how that was supposed to work but that's the story. What he did have, in addition to his tremendous enthusiasm and love for Rushden Town, was his motorbike!

In an era of very few motor cars, Cyril's trump card was his bike. He worked in the shoe trade in Rushden but his evenings, weekends and holidays were spent chasing after players – on his motorbike. He was born and lived in Rushden all his life. His home was a sanctuary for his players. Those from afar would live in the family home for a short time until Cyril got them fixed up with their own accommodation.

His son Ron who still lives in Rushden tells the story of his father, who like so many people in those days, could make shoes from scratch and often he would rise at 5.00am on a Saturday morning and make a pair of football boots for a player whose boots were too old or had no money. On one occasion, Cyril simply could not raise a proper team but somehow chased around Rushden and cajoled anyone he could find from the local amateurs to fulfil the fixture. They lost 18-0 at Wisbech!

It is reputed that he once travelled to Northampton to sign a certain Colin Lyman, but there was a hitch. The player in question advised Mr Freeman that he would love to play for Rushden but he didn't have a decent pair of trousers to travel on the bus from Northampton to Rushden. "No problem" – and Cyril was back an hour later with a spanking new pair of slacks and the player signed on the dotted line. Colin Lyman later played for Tottenham Hotspur so Cyril obviously knew a player when he saw one.

However, Cyril was more famous for his long distance treks. In his one week summer holiday, Mrs Freeman would wave hubby goodbye as he travelled to the North East – a particularly depressing area with high unemployment. Through his contacts, he found and signed players who were desperate for work. He got them jobs locally, mainly at John White Footwear, and Rushden Town flourished. John Hindmarsh was a particularly good signing

# Ten of Diamonds

from that area. He worked at Marriotts the Builders during the week and earned ten shillings (50p) per match on Saturdays. Were those really the good old days?

Cyril died in 1949, leaving a wife, three sons and four daughters. Sadly, another son, Cliff, was killed in the early days of the Second World War. Of the other three boys, his eldest, also a Cyril, was well known in Rushden for his garage and car sales. I wonder if he kept his Dad's famous motorbike?

Ron will gladly tell stories of his bike rides around the country with his father. His daughters, Katie, Hazel, Hilda and Winnie, have all passed away, although Hilda was married to Eric Harrison, a member of the all-conquering Rushden Town side of Cyril's era.

Cyril Freeman left a legacy to Rushden Town which was almost impossible to follow. Times were changing, football was changing and nothing is forever. That's why it is so important to remember footballing adventurers like Cyril Freeman. Rushden & Diamonds Football Club has done just that, in the Corporate suite in the North Stand which bears his name.

\*           \*           \*           \*           \*           \*

Ken Ambridge I knew very well. He was my era. He now lives in Skegness, is still very active and I see him at least two or three times a year. He basically followed on from Cyril Freeman – a difficult enough task in itself but he pulled the Russians together during some very difficult times.

Ken had joined Rushden Town from Rushden Baptists and in his very first season one of the club's most important signings was Ted Duckhouse as player/manager.

Duckhouse, who had made his name with Birmingham City as a tough resolute centre half, had been with Northampton Town when he agreed to join Rushden Town, provided they could sort him out with a house and a job. The Russians were only a semi-professional club and therefore the players worked in the week and played on Saturdays.

The Rushden Town supporters club purchased a house for £900 – this was in 1952 – and also got Duckhouse a job with Swindall's, the coal merchants, so far so good.

However Ted had bad knees; something that had not been made clear at the time of the signing and not long afterwards, packed up playing altogether. He carried on as manager only, and eventually left the club after four seasons.

*Ken Ambridge*

Ken Ambridge tells the story of his departure and when they came to sell the house, all they received was £500 for it – a big loss at that particular time. He says they never got involved again with house purchases!

At a time when Rushden Town had more managers than they would care to admit, it was Ken who was always leading the way. Whenever anyone in local football talked about Rushden Town, it was not the manager they referred to but Ken Ambridge.

# Hospitality, Celebrities and the Emerald Isle

Apart from both Ken and myself firstly being secretary and then chairman of our respective clubs, we also served together on the management of the United Counties League for many years. It is true to say that in each capacity, Ken and I didn't get on particularly well. But times and circumstances have changed, the years have rolled by and now, as two old stagers, we have a drink together and reminisce – good pals now.

After all, there is no longer Irthlingborough Diamonds nor Rushden Town – just one big happy family now, but it certainly wasn't always like that.

Ken Ambridge was supremo at Rushden Town from 1952-1988, 36 years magnificent service. During this time, the Russians were United Counties League Premier Champions twice – 1963-64 and 1972-73 – whilst the Diamonds had three championship triumphs in the same period. Overall the match results were generally fairly even.

But Ken always considered that Rushden Town were the more senior club and I suppose in many ways they were. In his latter years at the club he became chairman but outside influences were at work and Ken called it a day in 1988.

So although there was a great rivalry between the clubs there nevertheless was a close connection.

As with so much in life, that is now all in the past. But as for guys like Ken Ambridge, their legacy remains at Rushden and Diamonds Football Club forever – and so it should.

\*         \*         \*         \*         \*         \*

Over the years, there has been a steady stream of footballing celebrities at Nene Park as guest speakers at the regular Sportsman's Evenings. Virtually all of the big names in football, dating back over the last 40 years and one beyond, have spoken in the Kimberley Suite at the Diamond Centre. They have included Sir Bobby Charlton, Alan Ball, Billy Bremner, Johnny Giles, Ron Yeats, Frank McLintock, John Charles, Jack Charlton, Jimmy Greaves and Bruce Grobbelar.

Dennis Law actually opened our 'Seasons Bistro' in 1998 before moving upstairs to the Kimberley Suite where he spoke most eloquently and passionately to 200 guests. Sir Stanley

*L-r: Neil Midgley, Max Griggs, Dennis Law, Ted Carroll.*

# Ten of Diamonds

*Max Griggs with George Best.*

*L-r: Max Griggs, Howard Johnstone, Mark Darnell, Sir Stanley Matthews.*

# Hospitality, Celebrities and the Emerald Isle

Matthews was another football icon from a totally different and bygone era, and although he didn't speak for very long, he commanded great respect from another large audience

Probably the biggest footballing name ever to visit Nene Park was George Best. The occasion was a complete sell-out weeks before the night but it was at a time when George was not altogether the most reliable at turning up for such events. Therefore Ted Carroll, who organised all of the speakers, decided to take his pal and another English football legend, Phil Neal, with him to London to pick George up and bring him to Nene Park in his car. Phil new George well and assured him that the Diamond Centre was a top venue, and so he came.

The Kimberley Suite was a buzz with anticipation and when George arrived and just walked in, there was a tremendous standing ovation. Neil Midgley, the ex-first class referee and then a top class Master of Ceremonies advised Ted to keep George short of alcohol during the dinner and subsequently George was able to enthral his audience. The first thing he said was, "I bet you didn't think I'd turn up!"

Here was a true world-class footballer who just by turning up, was capable of holding his fans in the palm of his hand.

\*            \*            \*            \*            \*            \*

In the spring of 1998, Brian Talbot asked the Board for their permission to have a pre-season trip to Dublin in that summer. Because of a very special relationship that Brian had with the Shelbourne director and owner, Ollie Byrne, the Irish club would basically finance the trip. How could we refuse?

*The lads leaving Stanstead, for Dublin.*

July is when many people take their holidays and it seems that for most of our directors, this was also the case. Quick to put my hand up, I was in fact the only director available – how very convenient.

# Ten of Diamonds

However I soon had a pal to keep me company and Ted Carroll and I flew off to Dublin with our first team squad. It was in fact my first visit to Stanstead airport, but more importantly and much more interestingly, it was my first visit to the Emerald Isle and in particular Dublin.

Our job was basically to be there to support Brian Talbot and his lads. The object of the trip from the playing point of view was for the lads to live together for four days in a training camp environment and play a couple of games. This was a completely new venture for us and Brian obviously wanted us to maintain our professional club mentality in all aspects.

So here we were in Dublin – a lovely city by any standards. The splendid architecture, world famous universities, the river Liffey and Temple Bar (but that's another story).

I must confess that Ted and I stayed in a very nice hotel while Brian Talbot and his lads stayed at the Dublin University, all in rather small rooms and not at all salubrious, but nevertheless this was all free thanks to dear old Ollie Byrne.

What happened was that basically the lads trained both morning and afternoon, except for the days when they had a game in the evening. Ted and I would just go along and watch, nothing thrilling about that, but the weather was nice and there were always plenty of laughs.

One morning we decided to have a game of golf and drove to St Margaret's golf club. "Good to see you at our club", was the lovely welcome. We enjoyed our eighteen holes on a splendid course and as we then went to the changing rooms before intending to have a drink at the bar, what followed was typical of Ireland.

Before we could leave the changing rooms, a voice shouted, "Oh, you're from England then? We will show you the way to the bar, in fact, you must have a drink with us".

Now you must bear in mind we had no idea who was speaking to us, nor had we ever seen them before.

Suddenly a gigantic, eighteen stone guy and his little mate emerged from the other side of the changing rooms.

Unfortunately I can't recall their names but these two fellows took us to the bar, bought all the drinks – no way would they let us pay for anything – and then when they had got us well pissed they then insisted on driving us back – not to our hotel but to the player campus at the university because as the big fella said, "We want to meet Brian"

This was completely the wrong direction for them to be going home – but no problem, everything in Ireland is **NO PROBLEM**. We were supposed to be taking part in a player's cricket match that afternoon and we were late. Apologies to Brian and the Irish lads who were then on their way home in the huge Mercedes 500 S Class.

During our car journey, the big guy enchanted us with a collection of stories. One I particularly remember is that as a race horse owner, he always visited Cheltenham every year for the Gold Cup. In the hospitality box there were eight Irish men over for the jolly and the steward, or whoever, delivered to the suite six crates of champagne. "Would you like me to open a couple of bottles?" he asked. "Then when the rest of your party arrive I will come back to open up and serve some more bottles", he continued.

"This is OUR party", the big guy said, "so you'd better stick around so you can open the rest of the crates because we are very thirsty lads".

The little guy told us that this lad, aged fifteen years, had just joined Nottingham Forest Football Club and although we were not absolutely certain of his name, Ted thinks that the lad would now be nineteen and made his first team debut this past season. We tried to contact them the following year but the club were reluctant to give us their telephone numbers – unfortunate but understandable.

The two games we played were against Shelbourne and Home Farm. Now Shelbourne had played in the European Cup in the preliminary round a couple of nights before against Glasgow Rangers and we played only against their squad players. Nevertheless we had an enjoyable match which we won quite comfortably.

# Hospitality, Celebrities and the Emerald Isle

*Shelbourne Club House "enjoying the Guinness."*

The boardroom at Shelbourne FC has to be seen to be believed. It's an old fashioned ground with a similarly delightful boardroom. Ollie with his manager, his brother and a couple of other guys then entertain you as only the Irish can. Now Ollie is an absolutely typical Irish host. His lovely lilting accent is complemented by a very laid back demeanour and as far as Ollie is concerned, everything will be OK on the night. I had never met him before but was immediately bowled over by his easy-going welcome.

Now Ollie's brother is something else.

First of all he does everything that Ollie tells him and our next encounter with him was at Home Farm. None of us were too sure just who Home Farm really were. They had recently added the word Everton in front of their name, but whether there was any connection with the Liverpool club, we were never able to establish.

We were given complicated directions on how to get to the ground which I believed belonged to another club – nothing in Ireland is ever straight forward. Eventually the driver of the coach, which again Ollie had provided for us, found his way to the ground.

The outside looked very rough indeed – all six feet high rusty corrugated tin sheets with a broken down old gate. What had we let ourselves in for?

The driver was uncertain where to park the coach and decided to see if he could find anybody. Brian said to him, "While you are in there, see what the pitch is like" – meaning obviously, is it good, bad or whatever.

The driver returned and announced, "It's grass, sir"

He looked quite puzzled when we all keeled over with laughter but that's the Irish. It sure enough was grass and pitch was as rough as hell. It had been cut that very morning with an old hand mower and six inches of cut grass covered the whole pitch. I really do believe it's the worst I have seen anywhere, even dating back to our old Irthlingborough Diamonds youth days of the late 1940's.

Suddenly Ollie's brother turned up. "I cut the pitch for you this morning, sir", he said to Brian. "Ollie told me you wouldn't like it too long, Sir".

# Ten of Diamonds

All one can say is that we played a game of football against a rather poor opposition and won 3-0. However one very interesting feature of the game was that Home Farm had an excellent young centre-half. I enquired to their manager about him and he said we could buy him for £30,000. "Thank you very much", I said. Incidentally, we later learned that both Arsenal and Southampton offered him trials, so he certainly had something – whatever became of him, I don't know.

The trip was nonetheless a huge success. Good tight discipline was maintained throughout although on one occasion when the lads were allowed out for half an hour at the pub near the campus, two of the squad were a few minutes late in returning; I seem to remember that fish and chips was the excuse given. Brian Talbot read the riot act and threatened to send them home the next morning. There were no further late calls!

The other amazing and pleasing thing I can remember about the trip was our fans that travelled to Ireland to give us their support. Why they even wanted to go to Ireland for just friendly games or how they ever found the Home Farm ground I'll never know.

On to Temple Bar.

For those that do not know Temple Bar, and I was certainly one of them, I must explain.

On our last night, the coach took us into Dublin and dropped us off at the end of the street which is Temple Bar. I suppose the area might be considered similar to Soho in London but without the night-clubs and strip joints. Instead, every building is either a restaurant or a pub, mainly the latter. In every pub there is live music. How they ever got licences from the Fire Department I will never know.

Every pub is jam-packed tight with people seven nights of the week – fifty two weeks a year. When I say packed, I mean shoulder to shoulder, standing upstairs as well as down. It is absolute utter pandemonium, but incredibly exciting – even for an old guy like me.

Brian Talbot had issued the ultimatum that anyone late for the agreed curfew time was in big trouble. No one was.

Our second Irish pre-season foray was exactly one year later. Again, Ted Carroll accompanied me and the only changes this time was a different university and a different hotel. Otherwise, the friendliness and generosity of the people remained exactly the same – superb.

I always laughed at the jokes at the expense of the Irish and I certainly loathed the violence of the minority. But unless you have been to Southern Ireland then you cannot appreciate their humour and genuineness which these lovely people exude.

We were met again at the airport by the laconic Ollie Byrne – our host par excellence – this is the best possible introduction to this fair city. Despite the seemingly lackadaisical pre-trip arrangements, everything turned out to be spot on and again nothing was too much trouble.

Our first game was at Newbridge Town, which was the home of Niall Quinn before the Arsenal beckoned. Newbridge is some thirty miles out of Dublin – a typically Irish town whose players and officials knew of our earlier exploits against Leeds United. Apparently Shrewsbury Town had been there the previous week and had not been best pleased with the facilities. The fact that Newbridge beat them probably didn't help.

These lads were no pushover, having lost only one game the previous season in winning their league. A spirited game saw us eventually emerge 2-1 victors. Again it was particularly encouraging to see a contingent of Diamond supporters arrive at this sleepy out-post and their bar takings must have been greatly enhanced. Accordingly our visit was turned into a VIP exercise with both sets of players and staff treated royally to a splendid after-match meal.

The coach trip back to Dublin saw Irishman Michael McElhatton in superb singing voice and as we approached the university campus, our coach driver added to the fun by signing off the journey with "When Irish Eyes are Smiling". What else do you need to bring a splendid evening to a close.

# Hospitality, Celebrities and the Emerald Isle

*Saturday night at the races. L-r: Dave Joyce, Ollie, BT and me.*

Training for the fit and medical rehabilitation for the wounded was the main daytime activity and everyone was kept busy. But Saturday night was greyhound racing night.

The whole party descended upon Shelbourne Park, thanks again to the generosity of our host Ollie. It was particularly a night to remember for Brian Talbot, who backed six winners from eight races. It was a tremendous fun night and Saturday in Dublin the people certainly know how to enjoy themselves.

Another beautiful off-the-cuff moment came when Ted Carroll and I walked through the lobby of our hotel and heard the strains of "The Rose of Tralee". There sat a family of guests with the old grandad singing away while his son played the accordian, mum and the rest of the family, including the little ones, were providing the backing – we simply stood entranced.

Sunday morning saw the teams sports quiz end in a blaze of glory for Mark Copper, Darren Bradshaw, Jim Rodwell and yours truly. In the evening we were off once again to play Shelbourne who had their full team on view this time and were too smart for us, and run out winners by 3-1. It was a disappointing performance and was not the ending we wanted to another memorable trip. However an hour or so in the enthralling Temple Bar area again cured our blues.

One final thought.

Immediately before the entrance to the university is a bridge that spans the main dual carriageway with cars racing in and out of the city. Ted and I had to cross this bridge to get to the university each day and were very moved with the plaque and other poignant farewells to disillusioned and desperate young people who had climbed the railings and leapt to their deaths. One can only assume that these tragic suicides were prompted by pressures encountered at the university or maybe because of drugs – or both. It was a very sad reminder of how fragile life can really be if despondency and despair take over. It really did put the losing of a football match into perspective.

*Relaxing at Dublin University campus.*

Our third and final trip to Ireland (at least for the time being) – the scenario had changed.

Our stories of hospitality were now legendary and family holidays by some of the directors were amended to suit the Irish trip. Our managing director Mark Darnell and sponsor Frank Langley made our official party into a quartet. The chairman and his son Stephen together with their ladies also joined us separately.

There is always considerable apprehension when fixing games up with Ollie Byrne. When I heard that Home Farm was again on the agenda, my heart sank. Secretary David Joyce spoke to Ollie a couple of times explaining our concern regarding their pitch.

"No problem", says Ollie.

"You said that last time", replied Dave.

"David, would I let you down? I fixed up a different, lovely little ground for you. Trust me"

So off we went once more to the fair city of Dublin with fingers crossed. The lads were billeted at the city of Dublin University Campus. They trained twice a day whilst Cardiff City, who were staying at the same university, played a game every day, but with no training. Jim Rodwell thought this a much more civilised idea.

With Brian Talbot deciding that Paul Underwood, Billy Turley, Simon Wormull, Michael McElhatton and Darren Collins were all not quite fit and therefore should not travel, this gave

# Hospitality, Celebrities and the Emerald Isle

the opportunity for some of the youngsters to make the trip – and with Andy Burgess and Gary Mills already in the party together with nineteen year old Michael Bertocchi, they were belated opportunities for three late replacements. These were nineteen year old Richard Butcher and the two babes of the party, sixteen year olds David Bell and Daniel Talbot.

Before the game against Home Farm on the Wednesday evening, we encountered our first major hitch. There was no sign of the coach and we had been waiting for one hour. The decision to order six taxis as a replacement was hastily made.

What happened?

As the first taxi arrived, so did the coach. Oh, the joys of Ireland!

For the Home Farm game, Ollie was as good as his word and we were not playing on the same ground as we had done two years earlier. The ground, on which he had arranged to play this game, belonged to the local garda which had superb social facilities – splendid tennis courts and an eighteen hole golf course. The football pitch however was not the best!

As always, the hospitality was superb and our police host said they had paid for EVERYTHING themselves to which I suggested the fines in Dublin must be the highest in Europe. As for the game itself, we didn't play particularly well and lost 2-1.

There was an amusing little incident the following day that centered around Doc Pepperman, who travelled with us on all three trips to Dublin. The lads were training on the playing fields belonging to the university, when the doctor came wandering along in his club tracksuit. He waved at the lads and sung out, "Everything alright, Ducky?", to physio Simon Parsell. Then he disappeared.

He was seen walking into a gap in the long hedge bordering the playing area, but he didn't reappear. Nobody took any notice at first as it was assumed that he had nipped into the hedge to relieve himself. After all, doctors pee just like anyone else.

The training went on for the best part of another hour and then one of the lads said, "I didn't see the doc come out of the hedge" "No", came the chorus reply. The possible thought regarding his non-appearance was the possibility of a fall or even a collapse.

"Hell, I hope not!", said someone. "I don't want to have to give the Doc the kiss of life!"

Anyway the lads went scrambling into the hedge as they sought out the missing doctor – just like golfers do when an errant hook or slice lands in amongst the bushes. Anyway, he was never found.

I say never, because when the lads were on the way back to the university buildings, there emerged the Doc all dressed up in blazer and tie. There were various questions fired at him but the general gist of it was "where the hell did you go when you went into the hedge – you had us worried" Well it was addressed somewhat differently to that, but that's near enough that I can relate.

The Doc looked puzzled but nevertheless pleased that so many people seemingly were concerned. "Oh, I knew a short cut back to the camp through the hedge. I thought I'd go and get changed for tonight's match". "But the match is tomorrow night", said Simon Parsell. "Well, I'll be ready for that then", said the Doc, and he walked past them like nothing had happened.

Which just goes to confirm our Doctor Pepperman is as zany as we all believed him to be, but we wouldn't change him for the world.

So it was Friday evening that saw us at Tolka Park, home of Shelbourne FC yet again. Two nights earlier Shelbourne had hosted a European Cup preliminary round tie against Rosenberg in front of ten thousand fans and apparently were very unlucky to lose 3-1.

For our game, Shelbourne fielded a side including only four or five players who had played in the previous game, the remainder were squad players. Nonetheless an excellent display from our lads saw us win 5-0.

Shelbourne chief Ollie Byrne presented our chairman with a delightful ornament of Molly Malone suitably inscribed in commemoration of our visit. As in previous years when

# Ten of Diamonds

*B.T. Ollie and me.*

they had made us a presentation, the 'S' was missing from the Diamonds but at least this time the 'H' was in Rushden. Nothing should surprise you with the Irish.

The highlight of the coach trip back to the university on that Friday night – well, Saturday morning to be exact – came from Jean Michel Sigere in his best pigeon English. Jean Michel entertained us with a speech on the professionalism and dedication required by all the players this coming season at Nene Park. He followed this up with a Bob Marley medley – it was quite a performance.

For our swan song, confusion reigned at Dublin airport on the Saturday morning for our return flight home. It was a right mess-up.

We had missed our flight but Brian Talbot showed great resourcefulness in obtaining a late switch to the next flight which was thirty minutes later. Quite incredibly, twenty four of our party of twenty six were able to be accommodated on this other flight. Unfortunately it meant two people missing out and Brian Talbot decided that he and son Daniel would have to suffer a further two hour delay.

That's what you call the captain being the last to leave the ship when everyone else is away safely – well done, Brian!

I can fully understand why so many English clubs visit Dublin every year for their pre-season warm-up games.

Will we return to the Emerald Isle again?

I hope so, one day.

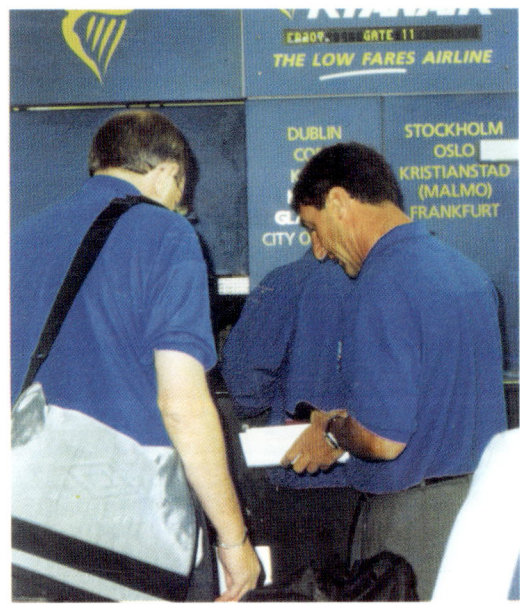

*B.T. sorts out flight problems with Dave Joyce at Dublin Airport.*

# 10
# EXPECTATIONS ABOUND

**THE month of January 1999 will always be remembered for the Rushden & Diamonds two epic encounters with the mighty Leeds United in the FA Cup 3rd Round.**

At the beginning of every season, clubs such as ours pin their hopes on reaching the 3rd Round and then drawing a Premiership club out of the hat – or to be more precise, a rotating bowl of numbered balls. Whereas our officials and fans were metaphorically 'over the moon', the Leeds manager David O'Leary must have let out a disgruntled, "Oh hell, that's awful!"

A top Premiership club against a non-league minnow means only one thing. Whilst they could justifiably expect to progress comfortably through to the 4th Round, they nevertheless would be well aware that a win would only be greeted with a "and so you should!" whilst the unthinkable would be met with derision and a thumping loss of revenue. But surely a multi-talented, multi-millionaire squad of players couldn't possibly lose to a club just seven years out of kindergarten – could they?

Enough of Leeds United and indeed the FA Cup; that was the furthest thought from our minds as we prepared for the new season. The all important question that everyone was asking was could the Diamonds improve on their 4th place in the Conference last season – but even more so, the 64,000 dollar question was were they good enough to win it?

BT had again been busy rebuilding a squad he believed could do just that.

Jon Brady, a right-sided player who he had coveted for a while, was bought from Hayes and Richie Hanlon from Welling. Richie had been at Chelsea and at one stage was considered to be one of their bright young starlets, but as so often happens, he was released and found himself at 19 years of age at Welling.

In addition, Lee Archer of Yeovil, an outside-left with a good turn of pace,

*Australian, Jon Brady in action.*

# Ten of Diamonds

*Richie Hanlon*

left-back Paul Wilson from Cambridge United and Michael McElhatton, who had surprisingly been released by Scarborough, were signings who were all on free transfers. Two other players, Carel Van der Velden and keeper Mark Gayle, came on three month loan periods. Van der Velden had been put on a strict dieting and weight loss programme in pre-season and I know that BT was very impressed with his svelte-like new midfielder.

With the new season imminent, BT spoke to the local Evening Telegraph saying:

"I believe we have an obligation to the public to entertain them, and that's what I intend to do. I've got the players now to play the type of game I want. Even if we start as badly as we did last year when we lost our first three games and didn't score a goal until the fourth, we

# Expectations Abound

will continue to play the same way. People will no doubt say that we can't win the League that way, but I believe we can. I'm sure we'll start as favourites. I don't know why because we only finished fourth last season. But as people think we have lots of money to spend, it's inevitable".

The Diamonds were initially installed as 3-1 favourites with Cheltenham and Woking, who had last season finished in 2nd and 3rd spots respectively, both at 6-1.

The scene was set – and the Diamonds went off like a train, winning the first seven games on the trot. It just couldn't have started better. Forest Green, Welling United and Barrow (new to the League) were not the hottest of hotshots to start off with, but that was fine for confidence building. Nine goals against only one conceded became 14-2 when in the following game, a newly promoted but high flying Kingstonian were hammered 5-1 on their own ground.

Adrian Foster (Fozzy) netted a dynamic hat trick – could this be the same player who had limped through the previous season without ever looking the answer to Brian's needs? Yes it was, except he was now fit and flying. Fozzy netted 11 goals in the opening 10 matches, two of which he had started on the bench. However it was to prove yet another frustrating season for him and by the end of the season he had only increased his league goal-scoring tally to 15 from 24 games.

Hayes were hammered 5-0 on the August Bank Holiday Monday at Nene Park but then we had two games, admittedly away from home, where we were decidedly fortunate to scramble home by 1-0 on both occasions. They were at Southport and Yeovil and in the latter game I thought Yeovil were miles the better side, but if you don't score, you can't win. Dover put an end to our run of victories at the eighth attempt with a 1-1 draw at The Crabble. We were not happy with that. However the Dover result was the start of a five match run which the Diamonds could only rustle up 3 points from a possible 15.

Without question the tremendous start had been nullified and Cheltenham Town were already showing that they meant serious business, with some fine displays. Brian had never been slow in ringing the changes or bringing in new faces to the club, if results were not favourable. He was always quick to spot deficiencies and he thought he needed another strong central defender and an attacker with flair. Although he had Collins, Foster and West on the books, injuries to one or the other of them was disruptive and there suddenly appeared that something was lacking in that department.

In a double swoop both Ray Warburton and Carl Heggs were signed in a big money transfer from Northampton Town, and optimism was again high at Nene Park. Warburton, who was skipper at the Cobblers, was surprised to be let go but money talks and the Sixfields club was short of cash. 'Razor' Warburton was to become a firm favourite with the Nene Park fans and would eventually be very instrumental in leading them out of the Conference.

Carl Heggs on the other hand was an enigma. He was a six footer, had pace, wonderful close control but was not a real goal scorer, although some ten weeks later that statement would be questioned when he scored the most famous goal in the club's history.

He played the odd game as a front striker but spent most of his time as a wide-left player who could beat two men easily with a body swerve and invariably lose it to the third! Assistant manager Billy Jeffrey, who had spent 11 years with Rushden Town, Irthlingborough Diamonds and then Rushden & Diamonds, became a casualty of BT's full-time regime. He had been Roger Ashby's assistant and key player with the Russians, then I had enticed him to join the Irthlingborough Diamonds in a player/manager role but he stayed one season and returned to Hayden Road. Subsequently he became Roger's right hand man when the clubs merged, but was not prepared to give up his 'normal' day job, which BT now required.

He has since done a fine job at Stamford Town, where it seems that all the younger lads who leave the Diamonds appear to go, and therefore he still had a good relationship with Brian. Brian gave considerable thought to Billy's replacement. He wanted someone with high quality coaching credentials and eventually decided on Terry Westley, who had been in

# Ten of Diamonds

charge of the Youth Academy at Charlton Athletic. More recently, he had been coach and then manager at Luton Town but had lost his job there. Terry was to be Brian's right hand man and what a super job he made of it.

In the 2-1 home defeat by Northwich Victoria, Carel Van der Velden dislocated his shoulder and never took part in a first team game again. He eventually joined Irish club Shelbourne where BT had close connections with its owner Ollie Byrne, but has since disappeared from the scene – I knoweth not where.

By the end of October we picked up 10 points from 4 games to seemingly get our title aspirations back on track. In the FA Cup 3rd Qualifying Round we beat Forest Green Rovers 2-0 and we were given a stinking away tie at Leatherhead. The game was only played at the second attempt on a mud bath after the original game being postponed due to a waterlogged pitch. Losing 1-0 until the very final minute, Ray Warburton crashed a header home to spare our blushes and take the tie back to the more plush surroundings at Nene Park.

*Terry Westley*

Just when it mattered most, the Diamonds came up trumps with a thumping 4-0 win and a 1st Round proper tie at home to Shrewsbury four days later. Shrewsbury was to be our yardstick. We could now judge our general progress against a reasonable Third Division side and although the FA Cup games can throw up some strange results, it was nonetheless pleasing to win 1-0 and deserve to.

However a second round away tie was not what we wanted but Doncaster Rovers, who were only relegated the previous season, would be our next opponents. Bath Town were sent back west after a 2-0 beating but it was then our turn to travel westwards to our old rivals Cheltenham Town as the month of December approached.

What is it about Cheltenham? Nice town, not the most welcoming bunch of people, but on the pitch they invariably held the upper hand. We didn't know it then, but they would continue to haunt us far worse. Anyway we lost again 1-0 at Whaddon Road and Colin West missed an all-important penalty! BT was on the transfer trail yet again. He still wasn't happy with his strike force and did a straight swap deal with Peterborough United, which saw Mequel de Souza join us, and Richie Hanlon sign for The Posh.

It might have seemed a strange deal but Hanlon, although an obvious goal threat from midfield nevertheless was not the workhorse that BT wanted at that time – but how that assessment was to change two years later!

# Expectations Abound

I recall very well seeing Mequel in his first outing at Telford. Not only did he score but he looked a wonderful player. There had to be something missing in his make up or Barry Fry would never have let him go – be it that Barry just loves doing deals. I was right, Mequel was a 'flatter to deceive' merchant. Division One player one week, and a Sunday pub player the next. But I'm jumping the gun again.

An FA Cup 2nd Round game at Belle Vue, Doncaster, in front of 5,400 fans desperate to see the Rovers start to reclaim a little of their past glories is not easy. They had ex-Liverpool star Steve Nichol at the back, literally walking through the game with real quality.

It was a dour affair and neither team looked like winning and neither did. There may not have been too much excitement on the pitch but there was loads of it – double thick – in the boardroom when the draw was made after the game. None of us could believe it – Doncaster Rovers or Rushden & Diamonds had drawn Leeds United at home!!

Ten days later on a cold December evening, 5,564 fans certainly had their money's worth, but any latecomers might have missed the frenetic opening five minutes when Doncaster's Mark Hume was sent off for a crazy two-footed tackle on Darren Bradshaw, and John Hamsher scored from a penalty for a foul on Heggs. Although Doncaster got an equaliser, two goals from Colin West and a tremendous diving header from John Brady saw us comfortably home.

Leeds United would be coming to Nene Park. No pre-season friendly stuff – this was the real McCoy. Tell me I'm dreaming.

However BT sounded a warning immediately after the game talking to the Evening Telegraph. He said,

"It's tremendous for the club naturally, because of the media attention it will bring. I've been involved in cup runs before and I know what can happen. I intend to make sure it doesn't happen here".

But it did!

Although we beat Farnborough 1-0 at home and on Boxing Day drew 0-0 at Stevenage, there was to follow after the two Leeds encounters a dreadful spell in the League.

On the last Saturday of 1998 we played Woking in what would be the final game before our game with Leeds United. On the one hand we were obviously looking forward to it so much and on the other hand the prospect could be terrifying. Then we were struck down with a major, major problem – we didn't have a fit goalkeeper on the books. Mark Smith and Mark Gayle both had spells in the first team but neither was fit for the games leading up to Christmas.

Then Terry Westley had an idea.

When he was at Luton Town, an American keeper named Ian Freur had a few good games. He was 6 feet 7 inches and not bad – so said Terry. But we had to find him. Eventually Terry found him, made contact and after the normal American Major League Soccer contractual complications, he came to England. He played in the Farnborough and Stevenage games, then was taken ill. He had a bad bout of influenza that made him most definitely unavailable for the Woking game on the Monday, five days before the Leeds match.

The only goalkeeper we had was 17 year old Steve Corry, our youth team lad. He had never even played in the reserves, but he had to play against Woking – what a mess! Not only was the defence magnificent with Corry totally protected, but the whole performance was top class for a Conference side.

Leeds United manager David O'Leary came to the game and was very impressed with the style of play that both teams displayed. We won 2-0 but it could so easily have been 5 – even O'Leary conceded that.

The next five days, there were regular bulletins on the health of Mr Freur, and they were not very good. On the Friday he got out of bed for the first time and whereas many would have said, "Sorry, but no way", Ian Freur to his great credit agreed to give it a go.

# Ten of Diamonds

The interest in the game was immense. A televised press conference was held at the Diamond Centre with every national newspaper present. Although Leeds declared that they had some injury problems of their own, there was no mistaking that the absence of striker Darren Collins and captain Ray Warburton from the Diamonds ranks was every bit as damaging. Meguel de Souza and Jim Rodwell came into the side, with de Souza deciding that this wasn't a Sunday pub game and at times created panic with his explosive pace.

An early goal by Leeds and then possibly a second and the floodgates would have opened – but it didn't happen like that.

Keeper Ian Freur was magnificent in the early stages and calmed our nerves, although in the third minute Fozzy had nodded fractionally wide with Nigel Martyn beaten. When Jonathan Woodgate upended Paul Underwood and received his second yellow card with 16 minutes remaining, the impossible was clearly on the cards. The fact that it didn't happen was only because Foster, with the goal nearly at his mercy, headed over the bar.

*Carl Heggs leaves Jonathan Woodgate in his wake.*

The final whistle blew at 0-0 and the expression on David O'Leary's face told the story of his relief more vividly than words. Personally I was glad in a way that we hadn't won – I know that sounds mighty strange but it would have meant missing out on the Elland Road replay in front of 39,000 fans.

The 4th Round draw for the winners of our tie was an away trip to Portsmouth. I settled for a replay on a bitter cold Yorkshire night and loved every minute of it.

So how does one describe such an evening of pure magic? As for us, little Rushden & Diamonds, it was a time for dreamers. Yet it was an evening we had earned – it was our 8th FA Cup tie of the season!

## Expectations Abound

The welcome from the Leeds United directors and all officials was absolutely top class. We were treated like old friends and equals. With twenty minutes left before kick off, I well recall Robert Langley and myself excusing ourselves from our hosts' table – we just had to savour the atmosphere of the stadium. The Leeds directors see it all the time but this was so special for us. We walked out into the stadium, full to capacity. It was like the Coliseum and we were about to be thrown to the lions.

*The unimaginable happened. Carl Heggs opens the scoring against Leeds United.*

Suddenly both teams emerged, side by side. It is worth recalling our side which was the same as the one that had performed so splendidly at Nene Park. It was Ian Freur, Tim Wooding, Darren Bradshaw, Jim Rodwell, Paul Underwood, John Hamsher, Michael McElhatton, Garry Butterworth, Carl Heggs, Adrian Foster and Meguel de Souza. I said a little prayer, I really did. "Please Lord, let us perform well". Nothing about winning.

Eleven minutes on the clock and the impossible happened. After an incredible scramble in the Leeds goal mouth, Carl Heggs scored. Pandemonium! Then reality took over, and the Leeds United players with it, Alan Smith twice and Jimmy Floyd Hasselbaink put us in our places. The game was up, and we woke from our dream.

From the 315 curious spectators against Bilston Town in our club's first ever game six years ago, to 39,000 at Elland Road, this had to be the ultimate. Throughout the whole country, people must have asked, "Who are Rushden & Diamonds?" Well if they didn't know, they certainly did now.

The final whistle ended the match but our players didn't want to leave the pitch. It would be a long time before they could experience this atmosphere again – if ever. When the euphoria subsided it was back to fighting our corner against our equals. I wondered then, if this occasion would have an adverse effect on the League battles yet to be fought – I was right, it did.

Not only did we take just 5 points from the next 5 games, but additionally this poor run also saw us knocked out of the FA Trophy 4th Round by Woking yet again. A 0-0 draw at Woking was acceptable but back at Nene Park three days later we had the kind of start we could only dream of with skipper Ray Warburton lashing the ball home in the first minute of the game. Sadly to say a below par performance followed and the less-than-2000-fans indicated how support can plunge when the results start to go haywire. The season that had started in a blaze of glory was in danger of dying a slow, lingering death.

Brian Talbot summed up the mood by saying, "I'm not making excuses. We got what we deserved last night and the players are understandably very, very disappointed. It's another time they won't get to Wembley".

What was making matters so much worse was that it wasn't just Cheltenham Town we had to be concerned about – it was neighbours and biggest rivals Kettering Town, who just couldn't stop winning.

The Poppies were on a roll and the thought of them beating us to the Championship and the Football League was frightening. We still had to play them twice so perhaps we could do something about it. We even considered a midnight mass at Nene Park to pray for help and divine intervention! Not quite true, but no doubt you get the gist of our fears.

Then we hit a winning streak; well, not quite a streak, more of a canter, when we actually put together three consecutive wins. For the opening ten minutes of the 3-1 win over Southport, Brian Talbot left his dugout and joined the fans on the Peter Debanke Terrace. It was a spur of the moment decision as he said, "I've enjoyed the banter they've had with me and the team. Football's all about having fun".

Really, Brian? Certainly he would never have contemplated such a move nine months later when the same fans were calling for his head!

Remarkably one of the more unfashionable clubs in the League, Hayes, was now mounting a strong challenge and their 2-1 win over a lack-lustre Diamonds side proved their worthiness. Diamonds had just three days to climb back on board as challengers and the visit of Stevenage saw the return to Nene Park of Carl Alford, who BT had released a few months earlier.

His old strike partner Darren Collins was in the opposite camp and back to his best. His two goal burst in an exciting contest won the day for the Diamonds and on the day, there was little doubting who looked the better forward. Nonetheless, Alford was leading the Conference goal scoring list, so he could therefore claim that BT was too quick to ditch him.

The win over Stevenage was the first of a six match burst back into the limelight. Four wins and two draws from these games hauled us back yet again into the race up the finishing straight. The away wins at Leek Town and Morecambe both by 3-2 were particularly pleasing as they preluded our next away trip to the cauldron called Rockingham Road. This away match against Kettering Town was vital for both clubs to pick up maximum points, but neither did. 5,039 fans saw a drab deadlock of nervy football which erupted in the second half when passion really took hold. Darren Collins was sent off after 65 minutes and the Diamonds ten men settled for a 0-0 draw.

It's always interesting to hear the differing viewpoints but more so than when it's a derby between local rivals. This was how Brian Talbot saw it:

"We've got to be pleased with a point because it means we go top of the table. But I thought we could have had three because we were the only team who tried to play football".

Peter Morris, manager of Kettering Town, said, "Now we'll just have to go to Nene Park in May and win there to make sure they don't go up"

That's neighbourly love for you!

# Expectations Abound

Another view of the game came from the provocative Poppies midfielder Paul Raynor who said, "We'll never have a better chance of beating them. Once they went down to ten men they just sat back and defended, which surprised me"

Really?

If the Kettering game was a big one, how big was the next one going to be? We had the slenderest of leads over Cheltenham but they had a couple of games up their sleeve and came to Nene Park confident that the 'Indian sign' they held over us would hold good.

I had always questioned the term 'six pointer' by saying that there are only three points at stake so how can it be deemed as a six pointer? Now I know.

The game had been hyped up to be a title decider, which it was never going to be as we still had six games after this one, but it was a very important and likely indicator as to where the Conference trophy might eventually be bound.

6,312 fans were inside the ground and apparently a lot more Cheltenham ticketless supporters outside clamouring to be allowed into Nene Park. We had allowed a generous, over the required allocation to Cheltenham, but their chairman remonstrated with our MD Mark Darnell over the unfairness of travelling from the West Country and not getting admission, be it that it was an all-ticket game and they didn't have tickets!

The game itself was tight, taut, tense – use whichever word you like but it looked like one goal could win it.

De Souza gave the Diamonds a first half lead and as the game progressed, that was exactly what it seemed would happen. Perhaps we were a touch fortunate to still be in front, but we were in front and fortunate isn't a word you use when you are desperate to win at any costs.

After 85 minutes, we started looking at our watches; I don't know why because the electronic scoreboard told us all we needed to know – we were still 1-0 up with the minutes ticking away. 4-3-2-1 minute left; it was going to be our year!

Then in the 89th minute, Cheltenham equalised and our hearts sank. Instead of three points, we were only going to get one point each – so much for a 'six pointer". Barely another minute passed and the win that had suddenly become a draw now became a disastrous defeat as Cheltenham scored again. Two goals in the last minute!

Like every other club, we have suffered defeats due to poor performances – poor refereeing – defeats when you've played so well. Never had we suffered a defeat so blatantly unkind as this one. The boardroom atmosphere was simply unreal. The Cheltenham directors had obviously become resigned to the fact that they were going to lose – I know we would in similar circumstances. They didn't know what to say to us and we certainly were unable to even talk about it. We were shell-shocked and I know it took me days to recover. The team never did recover.

Two days later on the Bank Holiday Monday, we dolefully set off for Woking. Perhaps it wasn't the end of our dreams but whereas a point at Woking would have been a fine achievement in another year, it simply wasn't enough. Although Cheltenham still had a demanding run in, the news that reached us was another win for the boys from Whaddon Road.

If that draw hadn't entirely killed off our Championship aspirations then the next game at home against Yeovil certainly did – we lost 2-1 and by now we were looking sorry for ourselves.

Three days later we won a trophy – the NFA Senior Cup, beating Raunds Town 2-0 on a bumpy Kiln Park pitch. It wasn't the trophy we had in mind!

The league season was simply petering out and the Diamonds were playing for pride, but there was just one last score to settle. Kettering Town were coming to Nene Park for the very last game of the season and there were still two 'ifs' to be resolved.

If Hayes, the surprise revelation of the season, did not win their last match and Diamonds could beat the Poppies, which was a distinct possibility, then Diamonds could

# Ten of Diamonds

leapfrog them both and finish runners up. Not exactly what they had hoped for but better than finishing fourth. But it didn't quite work out like that. Although Diamonds led against the Poppies, it was the visitors who ran out 2-1 winners to end a devastating season which had promised so much.

Cheltenham Town finished on 80 points with Kettering Town only 4 points behind. That really hurt! Hayes were third and for the second year running Rushden & Diamonds were fourth, 8 points behind the champions.

The Leeds United encounters had been memorable but few fans were that interested now. It was the league title and the ticket into the Football League that they wanted; but nobody has the divine right to anything in life, nor in football, and one must accept such disappointments.

Perhaps next season our dream would be realised.

# 11
# SECOND IS NOWHERE AND SO UNFAIR

**PRE-SEASON friendlies can be tame affairs. They are meant to ease players into match fitness without too much stress and strain. Well, that's the general idea but when one of the so-called friendlies turns out to be a revamped NFA Maunsell Cup clash against Northampton Town, then it suddenly takes on a much more competitive edge.**

So that's how it turned out at Nene Park on a scorching August Saturday with the Diamonds needing a real confidence booster to kick off their ultimate challenge for the Conference trophy they so dearly coveted in the approaching 1999-2000 season.

A Mark Cooper 7th minute header was enough to seal a 1-0 victory for the Diamonds and secure a trophy for their cabinet, before a ball had been kicked in anger in the Conference.

*1999-2000*
*L-r: M. Sale, M. Peters, M. Smith. B. Turley, D. Collins, M. de Souza. Middle: S. Berry, G. Butterworth, P. Underwood, K. Cramman, T. Wooding, M. McElhatton, J. Hamsher, C. West, J. Rodwell, C. Heggs. Front: S. Parsell, M. Cooper, M. Mison, D. Bradshaw, B. Talbot, R. Warburton, J. Brady, D. Town, T. Westley.*

# Ten of Diamonds

While Brian Talbot was obviously pleased with the performance and putting one over the county rivals, the Cobblers boss Ian Atkins saw it as a 'wake-up call'. The Diamonds had the long trek to Morecambe as their opening league fixture and whilst the North Western resort is a better place to visit in August rather than February, it did not provide the hoped-for three points.

Michael Mison and David Town, who had both done well in the pre-season games, nonetheless were somewhat surprisingly preferred to Collins and Mark Sale, who were on the bench. Sale, a 6 foot 5 inch giant, had been signed from Colchester United to give BT alternative aerial power, but when he and Darren Collins were introduced in the second half, the effect was minimal. I suppose a 0-0 opening draw away to a team widely tipped as a major contender was on the whole reasonable. BT summed it up by saying, "We want to be hard to beat, but I think we can be more inventive going forward". I agreed entirely; and so we were!

Our first home league game proved a storming affair against Kidderminster Harriers, who were now under the management of Dane and ex-Liverpool star, Jan Molby. A 5-3 win was the scoreline with two extra special goals from Michael McElhatton. At times we were scintillating and on other occasions downright sloppy.

Kidderminster looked a poor side and opinions were expressed that they would have a difficult season. Whilst they certainly had a difficult start, how wrong those assessments turned out to be as the season progressed.

Mark Sale and Darren Collins had now taken over the mantle of a strike force with obvious potential, and Sutton United were badly mauled and dismantled by 4-0 at their Gander Green Lane ground.

Darren was starting to look like the Collins of old with a brace of clinical finishes, but it was McElhatton (Macca) who was really on fire. A goal at Sutton was followed by another two on the Bank Holiday home games with Welling, who were well beaten by 2-0. BT's assessment was that, "I thought we overpowered them – we had 19 shots and they only managed three attempts on our goal". So far, so good. A win and two defeats with nothing very inspiring then followed, with the 3-1 home defeat by Woking particularly galling.

However, the next game was against our old rivals Kettering Town at Rockingham Road. Neither side did their reputations any great credit, but pride being so important on these occasions, I suppose the 1-1 scoreline was about right.

Mequel de Souza starting his first game of the season netted for Diamonds while Colin Vowden, their ace penalty taker, again did the business for the Poppies. David Town had lost his place quicker that he must have hoped and BT had decided to transfer list Carl Heggs – things were just not progressing as smoothly as he had hoped.

As so often happens, the old adage of "When the going gets tough, the tough get going" applied to the Diamonds in their next trio of games. All were hard fought – all were won by the odd goal but the tough resolute commitment paid dividends and victories over Hednesford and Altrincham away set up the Diamonds for the game at Nene Park against Kingstonian, which they won 1-0 thanks to a magnificent strike by none other than Darren Collins.

The three wins had seen us leapfrog back to the top with Kingstonian just one point off the pace. Sutton United, who had conceded four goals against the Diamonds in an early season league game, had another four blasted past them, with Macca in tremendous form with yet another two from midfield. It was hard to believe that Sutton was competing in the Conference, so woeful was their form. What a shock they had in store for the Diamonds later in the season, when they were to meet yet again in another cup competition.

As a side issue to the main footballing purpose of winning first team matches, our Youth Section was taking shape nicely under the direction of Jeff Vetere. We had collected together a bunch of young lads from various parts of the country aged 16-17 years who were now to live in Irthlingborough together in apartments which had been purchased by the

# SECOND IS NOWHERE AND SO UNFAIR

*Michael McElhatton and Darren Collins.*

# Ten of Diamonds

Irthlingborough Diamonds Trust. The money which the Trust had received when the Griggs Group had bought the whole area of land from them had been used in various ways for helping the football club.

The Trust had bought these apartments where ten of our Youth players could now live – which seemed a pretty good idea to me. In addition, a cottage in Irthlingborough, a 14-seater Youth Team coach and the playing field on the opposite side to the stadium on the A6 road had all been funded by the Trust. My colleague and co-director Robert Langley, together with John Spavins, an ex-partner of Grant Thornton the accountants, and myself were the three trustees.

Although we obviously wear two hats at times, there is only one direction in which they are headed towards – the Rushden & Diamonds Football Club. At the time of writing, the Trust is hoping to fund new offices and classroom accommodation for the Community section, which has grown at a great rate of knots under the guidance of Greg Broughton, and is still expanding.

As a prelude to the FA Cup 1st Round tie with Second Division Scunthorpe United, Diamonds won their fourth consecutive league match, winning 1-0 away at Scarborough and the question was could they make it five in a row in the month of October. You bet they could!

Well, the bookmakers certainly thought so, and the Diamonds didn't disappoint as they simply blew away the Football League side 2-0 in front of 4,112 fans. A Ray Warburton header immediately after the interval and a John Hamsher penalty 15 minutes from time saw the home side celebrating their passage into the 3rd Round of the FA Cup for the second time in 1999. (As you may recall, Leeds United was in January of the same year).

Amazingly, what followed was probably the worst performance and defeat the Diamonds had experienced under BT's guidance. A 5-1 defeat at Yeovil is bad enough anytime but when the Diamonds boss had turned down a request of a change in kick-off time to allow the Yeovil fans to watch the Euro 2000 clash between England and Scotland, then he was certain to get some stick, and he did.

What was worse was that when Brian went across to apologise to the 100 or so of our travelling fans, abuse was hurled at him. As he said at the time, "Everyone to a man was poor. There are no excuses at all. Warren Patmore ran us ragged".

Where October had been a great month, November was poor and that's allowing for the fact that we moved into to the 3rd Round of the FA Cup by beating Ilkeston Town after a replay and sneaking through to the 3rd Round of the FA Trophy with a 1-0 win at Nene Park against Havant & Waterlooville who were two leagues lower in status.

Another home defeat 1-0 by Telford was not good but then followed a five-star performance away to Hayes 5-0 which the Diamonds hoped would give FA Cup opponents Sheffield United something to think about – it certainly did.

Bramall Lane, with a Sunday lunchtime kick-off is like Yorkshire without the roast beef but one soon forgets the time of day when kick-off comes. Another tremendous FA Cup result for the boys from Northamptonshire. Why, oh why, can't we hit a good vein of consistency in the league where it really matters? True, it was a rather soft goal from Jon Brady and a Billy Turley penalty save that got us the 1-1 draw, but most neutral observers thought it a fair scoreline.

Whilst we were all concentrating on the replay at Nene Park and contemplating Christmas a week or so later, tragic news hit the club. Mark Sale was battling cancer.

The striker had made only eight first team appearances and BT speaking to the Evening Telegraph said, "When he came here he didn't know he had the illness. We pushed him in training and he was always feeling tired. We just thought it was down to fitness. Now we know the reason, maybe people who were giving him a bit of criticism will be sorry for what they said. He will get a lot of support from the football club and certainly from me. He's a lovely man".

## SECOND IS NOWHERE AND SO UNFAIR

*Mark Sale*

On a personal note, I had a so-called fan telephone me two or three weeks earlier and slag off both Mark's performance and the club for signing him. I hope that fan reads this and remembers the conversation!

Focussing all our attention back to football just three days before Christmas, 6,010 fans packed Nene Park for the FA Cup 3rd Round replay against First Division Sheffield United.

With the score locked at 0-0 after 90 minutes, Denny gave the Blades the lead 12 minutes into extra time but skipper Ray Warburton headed the equaliser three minutes later and after the allotted 120 minutes, it was going to come to only one thing – who could keep their nerve in the penalty shoot-out.

Ten spot kicks crashed into the back of the net – it was machine gun practice! 5-5. Someone had to miss sometime, and ironically whereas at Bramall Lane the Blades keeper Simon Tracey had let Jon Brady's equaliser slip beneath him, it was Tracey who saved Brady's penalty this time. Marcus Bent then scored to make it 6-5 and the scenes that followed were a replica of a final win at Wembley itself.

Back to reality with three league games on the trot which registered only 4 points from 9, and then a tense 2-1 win at Bath City kept the Diamonds FA Trophy hopes alive and a passage into the 5th Round. The dream of a league and FA Trophy double was still on the cards but that's all it was to be – a dream.

Elation and tragedy then followed hand in hand.

After celebrating a stunning 6-0 home win over Northwich Victoria and a goal for new loan signing David Lowe, not to mention two more from Macca, the midfield goal snatcher, the roof fell in! Martin Aldridge was on a three month loan from Blackpool and had been on the bench against Northwich. Only a fortnight before he had scored on his debut at Bath – now he was dead!

He had been killed when driving to his parents home in Northampton after the Nene Park game. One witness said, "The Peugeot

*Martin Aldridge*

105

# Ten of Diamonds

(Martin's car), was literally in half. The back end of the car was 40 yards away from the front end. It was a nasty, serious accident".

Diamonds boss BT said, "It's a shock and a sickening blow. This tragic accident puts life and football matches into perspective".

His car had crossed the carriageway and collided with another car travelling in the opposite direction. Footballers paid a very special tribute at Martin's funeral where scores were unable to get unto the church service. It was so sad and all so unnecessary.

A forgettable replay win over Billericay saw us again reach the FA Trophy 5th Round and then our league form picked up over the next four games when we collected 10 points from 12 on offer. Darren Collins had reached a tremendous 150 goals landmark for the club but it was Mequel de Souza who scored the solo goal of the season at Doncaster to sink the Rovers.

Another striker to take centre stage was David Lowe, a Liverpudlian who broke the hearts of the Merseyside club Marine in Diamonds 1-0 home win which took them through to the quarter finals of the FA Trophy. I really believed that this would be our year in this competition, particularly when we were drawn away to Sutton United – bottom of the Conference and already having been smashed for eight goals in two previous encounters.

A win at Kingstonian and then a big game at Nene Park against Yeovil followed. Michael McElhatton's world fell apart that night when he was stretchered off with a very nasty knee injury which turned out to be much worse than expected. Now two years on he is still struggling desperately to overcome the various operations he has suffered. His wonderful season ended that night in the 1-1 draw and as it eventually transpired, his whole football career as well.

Sutton United should have been the proverbial 'piece of cake' for Diamonds to gobble their way into the FA Trophy semi-final. But football isn't like that. Facing relegation from the Conference, Sutton lifted their performance to a height hitherto unchartered and only a Jim Rodwell equaliser saved the day for the Diamonds – score 1-1.

No problem, a replay at Nene Park would soon send Sutton packing, but it didn't. In a sub-standard performance , the Diamonds capitulated to a side who had forgotten how to win. Somehow they remembered in time and Diamonds had no one to blame but themselves in losing 3-1.

The first half of the double was now gone!

Irony was heaped upon irony as Sutton United had to visit Nene Park yet again in a Conference league game only four days later! As in two previous games prior to the FA Trophy battle they conceded four goals yet again as Diamonds triumphed 4-0. Sutton were now in the semi-final of the FA Trophy and were facing almost certain relegation. As for the Diamonds, the burning question was could they still catch Kidderminster who were now really forcing the pace.

Inconsistency, which had prevailed all season, was to continue through to the finish.

There were 11 league games left, of which 7 were at Nene Park. We figured that we had to win every home game and thereby pick up 21 points. We were also to play Kidderminster away, which if we could win this vital game would not only add another three points to our tally but at the same time ensure that Kiddy's charge was halted. Had it turned out that way then we actually would have been the Conference champions but winning matches on paper is very easy.

The other three away games were at Woking, Southport and Welling of which we didn't necessarily need to pick up any points if our analysis of the other games proved correct. How wrong we were!

In reality, we beat both Welling 3-0 and Woking 3-1 away but our home form was so poor that the tally of home points totalled only 10 from 21. It is correct to say that our performance and defeat at Kidderminster by 2-0 was crucial and lacking in quality but as we were to lose the league championships by 9 points (Kidderminster 85, R&D 76 points), then if our home

## Second is Nowhere and So unfair

form had been better, I still believe that Rushden & Diamonds would have been crowned champions.

In those seven league games the only two wins were against Altrincham 1-0, who were to be relegated for the second time in four years, and our old rivals Kettering Town 2-0. Four home draws with only one goal scored was the real catalyst for our failing. The killer punch was delivered by Morecambe on an early April evening at Nene Park. Their 2-0 victory was sealed by a goal from Justin Jackson which won him the Conference Golden Boot for the league's leading goal scorer.

It also confirmed to BT that here might be the player to lead us out of the Conference the following season, and this was to prove to be the case. As for this season, we now knew that the best we could achieve would be the runners up spot.

The Kidderminster game earlier in the run-in had proved to be something of a watershed for Brian. Darren Collins hadn't been really fit for a long time and he was only a shadow of the player of 18 months earlier. David Town, a really lovely lad, never realised his potential while David Lowe's 3 month loan period had expired. We had to offer him a contract for the remainder of the season plus another year.

At 35 years of age, Brian was not convinced that he was the answer, particularly if we had got promotion. So Lowe went back to Wrexham and we were another striker short. Another missing forward was Mark Sale who had been out since before Christmas battling against cancer, and with very little options left, BT decided to play Michael Mison up front leading the attack.

It was difficult for the lad, and it didn't work well, although had his effort gone into the net instead of being miraculously hooked out from under the bar with the score only at 1-0 – then who knows!!

A section of the Nene Park fans were now gunning for the manager and demanding his dismissal. However not only were the Board NOT going to concede to the fans demands, we actually believed that Brian was the right person to take the club forward – and so it proved.

The runners up spot was the highest position that the club had achieved in the Conference but finishing second did not warrant Football League promotion – something that has now been rectified for the 2002-03 season. I felt that Mark Lea, the local Evening Telegraph sports reporter covering our last game of the season summed it up perfectly.

He said, "The best ever finish of second place, plus the memories of two cup runs highlighted by the heartbreaking exit on penalties to Sheffield United makes a mockery of calls for Talbot's dismissal. Whatever the minority who would prefer a new boss might think, he will still be in charge next season chasing the dream of promotion. And quite rightly so, because only the cruel system of 'winner takes all' in the Conference has provided the thin dividing line between success and apparent failure. Talbot is the right man for the job and Diamonds will be back again next season leading the fight for a spot in the Nationwide League".

Quite right and well said Mark

Stability and staying power are absolutely essential if a club is to progress along the right lines – as a club and as a Board of Directors, we felt we had both.

# Ten of Diamonds

*Max in training. Preparing for the final assault on promotion to the Football League.*

# 12
# FOOTBALLING TRIPS CAN BE FUN.....well, most of the time

**WHETHER you are a fan on the terrace or a director of the club, supporting your team on away trips is a must.**

Sometimes the distance might be offputting, the weather may be foul, the team's form is possibly awful – but you just have to go. How you travel is obviously a personal choice. The two separate Supporters Clubs of the Rushden & Diamonds Football Club both run coaches to every away game, while numerous fans just get together and travel by car, regardless of the distance. These are the true football fans who support their teams the length and breadth of the country.

As for myself, I am part of the Sharan Gang, named as such simply because there are seven of us who travel to all away matches in a Volkswagen Sharan People Carrier. Club Secretary David Joyce doubles up as our regular driver and the co-pilot in the front seat with all the leg room is Mark Darnell, our MD. When you reach such elevated positions, then you always get the best seats!

The other renegades in our party are Chris Smith, Ted Carroll, Frank Langley and last season we were joined by the new Diamonds director, Howard Johnstone. Now I always am at left-half – in other words, occupy the left seat of the middle trio. Everyone keeps the same seats – it's a ritual – similar to playing in the same position in the team each week.

When you are travelling long distances in such a confined area it is imperative that everyone gets on well together and it must be fun. I look forward to every trip, knowing that the banter will often be unrepeatable and that our lunchtime stops are likely to be outrageous. Naturally some trips are more memorable than others, but without question, all are good humoured.

It can sometimes depend on our destination, the quality (or otherwise) of the topics discussed, the TV programmes watched or anything else that we can find to argue over. The outward trips are invariably lively, the homeward ones usually sleepy – particularly if we lost! For example in our Conference days, a trip to Hayes could never compare to, say, Hereford, although we nearly always won at Hayes but never at Hereford.

In particular the trips to seaside resorts such as Morecambe, Scarborough and Southport were invariably amongst the best, but now we are no longer in the Conference, we are unlikely to be going to these resorts anymore – or at least if we do then hopefully it will either be in the FA Cup, or that they have been promoted to the Football League.

All of the three resorts I've mentioned had a nostalgic flavouring and glimpse of bygone eras, but all had a charm of its own. So let me try and give you a taste of some of the places we visited, some of the people we met and some of the things that happened to us, in supporting the Rushden & Diamonds Football Club.

# Ten of Diamonds

*Chris Smith*

\*       \*       \*       \*       \*       \*

Morecambe is a rather sedate North West resort with a question mark over it being classed as seaside. If you want to see the sea, you either must have some damn good binoculars or an aptitude for walking on wet sand for a mile or so towards Ireland. I didn't bother with either.

However, Morecambe is where I learnt to line dance – or that's the story Chris Smith tells. It was November 1998 and late autumn is not the best time to see Morecambe. We arrived at the hotel rather late and dined immediately, and about eleven thirty I decided I would take a walk. There were no takers for my request for company so I set off alone.

Several of the hotels along the sea front were already closed but one that immediately caught my eye was ablaze with light. I seem to remember it was the Headland Hotel and as I approached the large front window I could see several lines of ladies all dancing in unison to loud music. They spotted me straight away and several waved, welcoming me inside to join them. Now I may be game for a laugh, but me amongst fifty ladies? No thanks. I waited for a few minutes, waved back and then left. When I got back to the hotel around midnight, I told my story. Nobody quite believed it until the next morning.

The Morecambe weather was hardly bracing but nevertheless, after breakfast we decided to have a good brisk walk. We eventually came to the line dancing hotel.

"That's the one", I said.

I think it was Frank Langley who said, "What's more, Tony, they're all still dancing" – and they were!

## Footballing Trips Can Be Fun

This was about ten thirty in the morning and sure enough the gals were still strutting their stuff all over again. They spotted me amongst the lads and waved all friendly like. "So who's telling the truth now?", I said.

From that moment, the myth of Morecambe and my line dancing prowess was born and the story has been embellished by Chris ever since.

*             *             *             *             *             *

On my first visit to Scarborough I was pleasantly impressed. Our base was the Crown Hotel situated on the South cliff overlooking the beautiful crescent bay. The hotels are large and plentiful and I'm sure that in the real glory days of Scarborough, the town in the summer season would have been alive.

*L-r: Peter Phipps, Frank Langley, Tony Jones and Chris Smith at Scarborough.*

The Grand Hotel, which we visited on the Friday night before the match, was a wonderfully imposing building and must have been the 'crème de la crème' of sophistication in its heyday.

Someone likened it to being in a time warp but the gentry who must have flocked to Scarborough at the turn of the last century are long gone. Sadly, the interior of the hotel is now very dated and the ballroom was home to a temporary boxing ring where Paul Ingle, who was predicted to be Britain's next world champion, trained daily.

Saturday morning dawned and telephone calls to Northamptonshire told us that it was raining 'cats and dogs' – but not so in Scarborough. We had plenty of time to spare before the game and therefore a trip was planned. We headed out across the moors to Heartbeat country and the village of Goathland, or 'Aidensfield', to use its television name.

# Ten of Diamonds

*The Sharan parked outside the Goathland Hotel, better known as T.V.'s 'Aidensfield Arms'.*

We didn't see Mike Bradley or Claude Greengrass, but we saw the local pub, garage and stores. The Aidensfield stores were in fact a Heartbeat souvenir emporium. Ted Carroll duly purchased a six quid throwaway camera and the results – heaven forbid – appeared in the next home match programme.

Driving back over the moors, we spied Claude Greengrass's cottage nestling below us in the valley. Throughout the journey it was a laugh a minute and the only serious bit was the ninety minutes footie – now that was really tense. Hardly a thriller, but a 1-0 win away from home is always an excellent result.

I thought that Scarborough's McCain Stadium had a lovely feel about it and perhaps it was synonymous with the town itself. The hospitality and friendliness was like no other club in the Conference and top man and vice chairman was Trevor Milton, for whom nothing was too much trouble for this genial man.

Whilst we were there, the local newspaper carried a story of Scarborough Football Club being taken over by yet another multi-millionaire businessman, and with it came the promise of funds for new players, so perhaps our visit was well timed. I don't think it ever quite happened this way and Trevor Milton went to Doncaster Rovers, and Scarborough are still struggling.

The journey home was a long one but we had secured our three points, which always makes such trips much more enjoyable.

\*            \*            \*            \*            \*            \*

The town of Southport was probably my favourite place to visit. It is where the majority of Liverpool and Everton footballers choose to live. The town has lovely large houses, big turn-of-the-century hotels, Birkdale golf links and of course Lord Street with its classy shops and a splendid Victorian ambience. I found Southport to be rather regal and yet somehow quaint.

## Footballing Trips Can Be Fun

That is hardly the word that Diamonds Safety Officer and fan Barry Wills would use. Back at the hotel after a heavy night out, Barry just couldn't get his key to open his bedroom door. He had been told not to make too much noise in case of waking up the players. It was very late, he was frustrated and tired, so he slumped to the floor outside the bedroom and was woken by a chambermaid early in the morning. Needless to say she opened the door without any problems. Barry had been asleep outside his bedroom for over three hours!

At the same time, club photographer Paul Redding, who is a rather big lad to put it mildly, didn't go to bed until 5am. He immediately clapped out on the bed stark naked as soon as he got into his room. Around 11am, another chambermaid (at least I hope it was another one) found him lying on the bed like "a beached whale" – his words, not mine. Quite apt for Southport, where again the sea is miles out from the promenade. I said to him, "What did she say or do?" She said, "OH MY GOD!", turned, and ran out of the room as quickly as possible!

\*     \*     \*     \*     \*     \*

Whilst I would never put the town of Dover in the same league of resorts as others I have mentioned, it nevertheless was always an interesting trip and place to visit. So what did we think about our trip to the seaside town of Dover?

I can't call it a seaside resort because Dover is simply a working port. Though we didn't see a single bluebird, the white cliffs were still imposing and Vera Lynn's image lingered on. But Dover is never likely to figure on any TV holiday programme, as it is simply a link to the continent. The tunnel, the ferries, the hovercraft and SS Saga Rose for the golden oldies are its high spots.

On this particular trip, we arrived at about 6 o'clock. The Churchill Hotel was our base and the picture of Winston greeted us in his bulldog pose – we will need that spirit tomorrow, I thought.

Peering out of my bedroom window the next morning, my worst fears were confirmed – rain, rain, rain. It was Valentine's weekend, so gifts for 'her indoors' were a must, and a shopping trip to Folkestone took on a new meaning.

Shopping completed, it was soon back to Dover for the game. Chris Smith was constantly assuring us that the weather would change and the sun would shine. Well, he was bound to get something right sooner or later and sure enough, the sun came out.

Dover's ground at the Crabble is a tidy little ground and the pitch initially looked good, but soon resembled a Point to Point after five races, as divots were flying everywhere. The designated kick-off time was delayed ten minutes to allow the crowds queuing outside to get inside, and the two thousand nine hundred attendance was more than double their normal gate. I guessed that another boat-load of asylum seekers had arrived just in time. The name and fame of the Diamonds was obviously spreading.

\*     \*     \*     \*     \*     \*

For me, our FA Cup trip to Brighton was always going to be a nostalgic return to all my yesteryears. Brighton was where my wife and I spent our honeymoon and many other lovely holidays. Therefore, visiting the number one Sussex resort, albeit for a football match, was something to look forward to.

The approach to the town was as lovely as I always remembered it to be. Preston Park, beautiful gardens and large attractive houses all lead into the heart of Brighton. I always thought it was one of the more classy seaside resorts and on this cold but sunny winter day, it certainly lived up to its reputation.

# Ten of Diamonds

We checked into our seafront hotel at around 3.30pm and within twenty minutes were out walking the promenade. Little did we envisage that it would be midnight before we returned – no problem when you're having fun.

Our first port of call was the Palace Pier, which proved surprisingly pleasant and in good nick. Not much doing today, but it was December! So into The Lanes, a splendid reminder of Old Brighton, with its antique shops, jewellers and pubs. At this point, our walk, bracing though it was, took on a different role. We were getting colder and thirstier and a little hostelry was needed. The sun had gone down and it was now quite cold so a gentle warming snifter (or was it two?) helped our recovery to continue our exploration. Suddenly, O'Neill's Irish pub confronted us. How could we resist?

We didn't.

By the time The Cricketer's was discovered, it was nearly 7 o'clock and no point in returning to the hotel. A splendid Italian restaurant called Bartons was across the road. That will do nicely for the remainder of the evening.

Saturday morning dawned (well, sort of). Looking out of my bedroom window, I immediately saw a white-clad figure running along the promenade. Even through bleary eyes I could detect it was our team boss pursuing his normal fitness routine – oh to be as fit as BT!

Another cloudless sky, and with the sun on our backs, we took a final stroll along Brighton's busy seafront. Hotels might be changing hands and their names also, but no question, Brighton looked very buoyant. Down a side street I rediscovered the old Hippodrome where I first saw Frankie Vaughan some 40 years ago. Now it's a bingo hall. However, The Rock Shop provided us with a pleasant surprise. Its genial owner turned out to be

*B.T. in training mode.*

Chris Cattlin (ex-Coventry City defender) who was manager of Brighton from 1983-1987. Could Brighton rock really be that expensive? No wonder he packed up football and became a rock entrepreneur.

Now it was time for the serious stuff at Albion's Withdean Stadium – our first and hopefully last visit to their temporary home. Having lost the Goldstone Ground in very unsavoury circumstances, the fight back by the club saw them ground-share at Gillingham for a couple of seasons. The new club directors are desperately hoping their application for a new ground will be approved. If it's not, then there could be big problems now that the club has reached Division One status. Sky TV had covered the game live, so our early departure from the FA Cup was cushioned by a nice fat fee. It made our weekend on the south coast even more pleasant.

\* \* \* \* \* \*

So far my recorded reminiscences have only touched on visits to the seaside but there are other splendid memories gleaned from trips to larger towns and cities.

# Footballing Trips Can Be Fun

Such a trip was another FA Cup tie, this time to Sheffield United where the Division One club was obviously apprehensive about facing a non-league club who had already made their mark against top opposition.

Despite recent turmoil, Sheffield United Football Club is steeped in history, and Fifties goal-scoring icon Derrick Dooley had now returned as chairman to provide the necessary stability. The Blades were also sharpened by a newly appointed manager, Neil Warnock, which is always a rejuvenation for a struggling club and a danger to their opponents.

Saturday afternoon is when football was always played but not necessarily anymore. Instead it was a journey to Yorkshire on a rain-lashed M1 on a Saturday afternoon for our appointment at Bramall Lane for a Sunday lunchtime kick-off.

Sheffield is a city of complete contrast.

Renowned for its steel industry, it is also a university stronghold and in recent times has achieved fame for the successful film, 'The Full Monty' – but more of that later.

Saturday nights out in Sheffield mean bars packed with young twenty-somethings plus a gang of middle-aged guys and one golden oldie – me. Irthlingborough and Rushden were never like that in my day. After bumping into ex-Diamond Guy Branston, who promised to shout the lads on, a decision was required – where to go for the night out. WOW was the place but what, and where, was WOW?

It was a nightclub on the outskirts of Sheffield and we had to leap onto a freebee bus to be whisked away to WOW. Boarding the bus with fifty singing, clinging revellers was bedlam, but interesting. An impromptu virtuoso strip tease performance at the front of the bus enacted by a ginger-haired, pallid young man was on the en route entertainment. Off came the lot – I mean the Full Monty. Good, clean, regular Saturday night fun in Sheffield where at least the girls cheered the performance, but I'm not exactly sure why.

A fifty yard queue outside the infamous WOW was enough to bring us back to our senses and we quickly returned back to base with our tails between our legs and had a sensible drink back at the hotel bar. On Sunday morning the rain stopped and Sheffield took on a different look. The itinerary was in place and we had to be at Bramall Lane for a 11.30am brunch. A Sunday 1 o'clock kick-off seemed strange, almost as if you should be somewhere else.

But not today.

This was FA Cup day where sometimes dreams come true and where only the day before some big clubs hit the dust (or the mud) and others just survived to fight another day. All big clubs playing non-league sides are on a hiding to nothing but for clubs such as ourselves we are grateful for such opportunities, and the splendid memories of Sheffield.

\*      \*      \*      \*      \*      \*

I met up with one of my footballing heroes of the past – Malcolm Allison – quite by chance in the unlikely setting of Doncaster Rovers Football Club.

Arriving at the Rovers ground at Belle Vue opposite the more famous racecourse, we were escorted to the welcoming boardroom. After only being in there a couple of minutes, I was told, "Someone wants to see you in the VIP Lounge".

Walking through into the sponsors and VIP Lounge, I immediately spotted my old mate Ollie Byrne talking with Brian Talbot. Ollie, who had generously taken us under his wing on the pre-season trips to Southern Ireland, had flown over for the Sunday, Leeds United v Manchester United encounter. Brian had then invited him to come a day earlier and watch us try and achieve a vital three points at Doncaster Rovers. Chatting away to Ollie I then noticed a face I recognised. Initially I couldn't quite put a name to it, but then the penny dropped.

The fedora and a large cigar were missing, but bedecked in a fur-collared full length leather coat was none other than Malcolm Allison.

# Ten of Diamonds

At seventy years of age, Malcolm was still as large as life and looked in good shape. A big man in every sense of the word, he still had that charismatic air about him that was so reminiscent of his Manchester City glory days. In their heyday, the management duo of Mercer and Allison was a real top of the bill act.

I walked across the room without thinking and shook his hand warmly. "How are you, Malcolm?" I said, as if we were old buddies. He must have thought, "Who the hell are you?!" "Fine", he replied. In fact he was very nice, particularly as he didn't know me from Adam. He told me he did a bit of scouting for Arsenal and was hoping to see the highly rated Simon Marples but unfortunately he was injured and not playing. With Malcolm was another Mancunian legend from the other side of the city – Alex Stepney – the old Manchester United goalkeeper.

The world of football occasionally throws up opportunities to meet such legends, which is very pleasant indeed.

\* \* \* \* \* \*

Liverpool is synonymous with two great football teams and The Beatles.

Unfortunately we were not visiting the city to take on one of the Premiership giants, but for an FA Trophy game against non-league Marine, who only a year before we had met at Nene Park.

This was new territory for us and we had travelled up on the Friday afternoon and were staying at the Wrighting Court Hotel, which was very nice.

After our evening meal we wandered into the lounge and sat having a drink, where a guy was gently playing country and western music. He wore a big cowboy hat – a kind of Hank Williams look-a-like. Over the next half hour, into the lounge came a succession of people, many in wheelchairs, others disabled and handicapped, all accompanied by carers and parents. The evening soon got swinging and it was not only remarkable but quite moving to see how these young people were reacting to, and enjoying, the dancing and sing-along atmosphere.

Initially we just sat at the bar watching and enjoying the mood of the party. I suppose there were thirty or so of them, and it was not long before we joined in the party. We danced with anyone who would dance with us – it was great fun. It was also a real reminder of what we all take for granted.

During the evening we got talking to a very nice couple who were there with their daughter. The man asked why we were there and we told him that we were officials of the Rushden & Diamonds Football Club and were playing Marine in Liverpool the next day. His eyes lit up and he said, "My uncle lived in Rushden and we used to visit him on many occasions. His name was Wilbur and he was a fishmonger in Rushden High Street". Although it is no longer there, we all knew it well – in fact it had an excellent reputation in the area. We had a truly lovely evening and they promised that they would look out for the result. It turned out to be a thumping 6-0 victory.

However the next morning was miserable – cold, wet and windy. We decided that the regenerated Albert Dock area seemed as good as anywhere on such a morning and as we parked the Sharan, we immediately saw The Beatles Museum.

We didn't know quite what to expect but were entranced by the subterranean cave-like atmosphere where the Beatles' music, memorabilia and films were on display at every turn. For anyone going to Liverpool, it's a must!

\* \* \* \* \* \*

Nearly every trip away provided something special and I could go on and on about the places we visited but I'll settle for just the few I have told you about. After all, life is all about memories and many memories are only special to the people concerned.

# 13
# CONFERENCE CHAMPIONS AT LAST

**THE splendid new Dr Martens Sports & Leisure Centre – incorporating the training centre for the players – was opened in the summer of 2000. It was a tremendous new addition and facility.**

BT had contributed considerably to the layout and design of the footballing facilities, which included four dressing rooms, de-robing room, boot room, rehabilitation centre, large gymnasium, offices, players' canteen and briefing room. The building was adjacent to the two training pitches and all that was needed now was a Football League club alongside it.

This was to be our fifth and final season in the Conference. That is a very easy statement to make after the championship has been won, but far from easy when at the start of the 2000-2001 campaign, the expectancy at the club was even higher and the eventual outcome was totally unknown.

However well a club has performed in a previous season, it is of little significance when you have to start all over again with no points in the bag. Having said that, if a relatively successful squad has been retained and a handful of key players are added, then hopes should obviously be high.

As with every club, old favourites eventually move on and new stars emerge. Two such figures who over previous seasons had been adored by the fans were the two Darrens – Bradshaw and Collins.

Bradshaw had been the classy lynchpin of the defence, of whom David O'Leary at the time of the Leeds United encounter said, "Where on earth did you find him?!". He was that impressed! Collins on the other hand was the aggressive striker who had put fear into the hearts of numerous defenders and scored 153 goals into the bargain. Both were still in the 24-man squad assembled for the start of the new season but both were to make only one league substitute appearance during the course of it. David Town, a small darting forward who had promised well but had not ever blossomed was another present at the start, but to make only one league start.

*Duane Darby*

# Ten of Diamonds

All were to leave the club in the relatively early stages of the season. Collins joined near neighbours Kettering Town for a £20,000 fee, Bradshaw moved onto Stevenage and Town followed the path of other Diamonds players a year earlier by signing for Boston United.

Another very nice lad and excellent utility player to leave during the season was John Hamsher. He had performed solidly wherever asked to play but he decided that his lack of opportunities meant that he ought to move on elsewhere and eventually joined Stevenage Borough.

BT had decided at the end of the previous season that he simply had to acquire two new strikers with proven goal scoring ability if the club was to go that extra mile. He considered many possibilities but eventually came up with a combination that was going to cost the club and the chairman in particular a lot of money.

Duane Darby from Notts County had a decent goal scoring record but would cost £100,000! He had been checked out carefully and was considered to be as good as we would get for that sort of money. The deal was done.

However the other half of BT's plans – Justin Jackson – was a different proposition. He had been on the non-league scene for a while before also joining Notts County. He did not

*Justin Jackson*

# Conference Champions At Last

get the best of recommendations from their ex-manager, who was an old mate of Brian's but he liked what he had seen of him and thought that his blistering pace would be a perfect foil for Darby.

More importantly he had scored a hatful of goals for Morecambe only a few months earlier but he was going to cost big-time by Conference standard. The most that had ever been paid between two Conference clubs was the £85,000 paid to Kettering Town five years earlier for Carl Alford. That figure was about to be blown out of the water. It was £180,000 or no deal, said Morecambe boss Jim Harvey, so with the chairman wanting Football League status and BT thinking that Jackson could deliver, the fee was agreed. It certainly was now or never!

At the end of the last season, Frenchman Jean Michel Sigere had looked lively if somewhat unpredictable and BT was hoping he would provide the necessary back-up to the new signings. BT was also dubious about Darren Collins' fitness and commitment, and together with Mark Sales' unavailability, it did mean that a lot rested on the shoulders of Darby and Jackson. They eventually played 38 and 40 league games respectively and in so doing meant that this was one department that Brian could safely depend on.

The other two summer signings were right full back Tarkan Mustafa from Kingstonian and Gary Setchell from Kettering Town. Both were out of contract. Mustafa was an ex-right winger who would now provide pace at the back, whilst Setchell was a strong left-footed utility player, which gave Brian options and cover.

Although not in the squad at the outset, Shaun Carey, a local Rushden lad who had been released by Norwich City, was to join after only one game had been played, and starred in 32 league matches. He was a very neat midfielder who had joined Norwich City from Rushden Rangers as a boy.

What better than Saturday 19th August at Nene Park in front of a crowd of 3,966 with the sun shining brightly. Would our new big signings shine as brightly?

Yes they would and the two second-half goals in our 2-0 win over the relegated Chester were provided by none other than Darby and Jackson. A tough match, but we were off to the start we needed and the four games in the opening month of August provided us with four wins. Eleven goals scored and only two conceded with Darby 4, Jackson 3 on the score sheet, was a dream start.

The Hednesford away win by 3-2 was far more impressive than the score suggested whilst the 2-0 win over newly promoted Dagenham, & Redbridge was a much tighter affair with Jim Rodwell missing a penalty at a crucial time of the match. The fourth game in that opening month was back at Nene Park and a 4-0 thrashing over Southport managed at the time by Mark Wright, was the icing on the cake.

Fixtures come thick and fast at the beginning of a season and with seven league games scheduled for September it meant that by the 30th of the month, over a quarter of the league games would have been completed. Much more important was the fact that by the end of September, BT's side had not been beaten. 9 wins and 3 draws meant that 30 points had been collected from a possible 36. Everyone at Nene Park was very happy indeed.

Whilst acknowledging that a team cannot win all its matches, it was nonetheless a little disappointing that of the four games played at Nene Park during this period, three were drawn.

Stevenage Borough had equalised in the dying seconds with a Ray Warburton own goal, Forest Green had survived a 90-minute bombardment without somehow conceding a goal and finally Kettering Town had fought a long rearguard action to hold on at 1-1.

To compensate for the six home points dropped, the four away trips to Telford, Scarborough, Woking and Kingstonian, all registered maximum points and a four point lead over Yeovil had been established. For our first ever trip to Leigh RMI at the beginning of October, I was in Spain enjoying the sunshine rather than howling Lancashire wind that was

# Ten of Diamonds

encountered that night. Well, I thought, I was enjoying the warmer Mediterranean climate as I went to collect my morning newspaper until I hurriedly turned to the previous night's Conference results – Leigh RMI 1 – Rushden & Diamonds 0.

There had to be a mistake, I thought. I had fallen into the trap of taking a win for granted – a dangerous pastime. The scoreline was correct and it was a disappointing first defeat.

Four days later yet another newly promoted club were the opposition and Boston United's first trip to Nene Park saw Duane Darby red-carded after 56 minutes for a forearm smash and the game ended in stalemate at 0-0. Darby had already fallen foul of the authorities in the Poppies derby game when he had allegedly head-butted Macnamara in the players tunnel at the end of another battle. In consequence, Duane had to face the wrath of both the Football Association and a Civil Court hearing – something that was to hang heavily over him for most of the season, and which eventually resulted in a fine, suspension and community service.

Events went from bad to worse for the Diamonds striker when in the very next game at Nene Park against Hereford United, he was sent off again following two cautions. Thank goodness his strike partner Justin Jackson was on hand to deliver the only goal of the game to ensure the vital three points.

On the recruitment front – but not a player this time – 39 year old Steve Spooner returned to the club as Youth Team coach, replacing Jeff Vetere who had become the Charlton Athletic European Scout.

Steve had spent 18 months at Rushden & Diamonds in the Southern League and helped get promotion into the Conference. He said, "When I came down for an interview, I pulled up in the car park and just couldn't believe it. I had not been back because I was still playing and never got the opportunity. I am just amazed at what's gone on since then. Apart from the set-up, everybody is always so nice and they have made my family so welcome".

Keep saying the right things, Steve, and you'll get on fine – and so he has, having now graduated into the First Team coaching job, vacated recently by Terry Westley who joined Derby County as Academy Director.

Terry, who had a short stint as manager of Luton Town, had joined the Diamonds from Charlton Athletic and immediately made a big impact with his coaching talents of which BT had more than once said, "Terry is good enough to coach at a Premiership club".

Our next game at Morecambe was always going to be tough. Surprisingly they had been struggling in the early part of the season but one would never have thought so by their performance in deservedly winning 2-1 and giving 'old boy' Justin Jackson very little to remember on his return trip to the ground where he had been a cult figure.

Jackson showed his humorous side about his partnership with Darby by remarking, "Duane's not doing me any favours though by leaving me half way through the games!" He added, "If I get 20 goals this season then I will be happy with that". So he should be, and yes he did get the 20 goals he mentioned.

The only incident really worth recalling was the 30-yard strike from substitute Sigere although I do remember Morecambe keeper and ex-Diamond custodian Mark Smith showing exuberant elation of having put one over his old mates.

Two cup ties were to follow and whilst initially they appeared to welcome back one of the fans big time favourites in Michael McElhatton, it was to be a return that would turn badly.

Macca had been out of action since the Yeovil game at Nene Park the previous March with a cruciate ligament injury. He not only played in the League KO Cup 2nd Round match at home to Stevenage but scored in the bargain. Four days later he was given the nod to start an FA Cup 4th Qualifying Round game against Grantham Town and what a game that turned out to be.

Grantham, two leagues lower in status, led twice in as ding-dong exciting a match as one could ever wish to see. Incredibly, Macca netted two goals to put Diamonds 3-2 up at the interval. It was vintage McElhatton and most supporters must have been delighted at the

## Conference Champions At Last

prodigal son's return and feeling that he could just make the difference in the long haul to the league title.

How wrong we all were, and what cruel fate finished his participation after 65 minutes and much worse – for the rest of the season!

The game itself was pulsating and after numerous twists and turns finished up 5-4 in our favour. The first round draw immediately after the game saw us having to visit Kenilworth Road against struggling Luton Town. Could this be the forerunner of another FA Cup saga?

No time to dwell on that, we needed to beat Hayes at Nene Park three days later which we did in splendid style by 4-0, with Sigere in as replacement for the injured Darby, scoring twice.

November was a disaster zone!

Four matches – two league and two cup competitions – all lost.

One of the cup competitions was of little importance and losing 2-0 at Barnet in the LDV Vans Trophy was no big deal. Losing 1-0 at Luton in the FA Cup 1st Round was obviously more disappointing but with Duane Darby still not fit, it was not altogether surprising.

However it was the league games earlier in the month that knocked our league chances backwards and sideways.

The Yeovil encounter at Nene Park would decide nothing in the final reckoning but we were desperate to get our noses in front of what was fast becoming a two-horse race. A crowd of 5,283 saw Warren Patmore open the scoring five minutes before the interval but Justin Jackson was on the spot to tap in a rebound from a Sigere shot that cannoned off Pennock and Diamonds were level. In the 82nd minute, Jon Brady was sent off for saving a certain goal with his hands and Darren Way shot Yeovil into the lead from the penalty spot. First blood to Yeovil !!!

Three more points went by the wayside but not without a tremendous struggle at Doncaster. Keeper Billy Turley was send off after 13 minutes for a last ditch foul which also resulted in a penalty kick. Stuart Naylor coming on to replace Turley as Wormull was sacrificed, picked the ball out of the net for his first touch. A 3-2 defeat meant that Yeovil were slowly pulling away from the Diamonds but worse was to follow in the first Saturday of December.

Dover has seen some reasonable results and performances from the Diamonds but not on this occasion. Earlier in the morning a gang of us, including our chairman, had walked along the top of the white cliffs of Dover, taking in the sea view and the constant comings and goings below us in the port area. Max had jokingly said that a bad result in the afternoon might mean him returning to the spot and walking over the edge.

Well he certainly got the bad result as our dreadful form continued. Billy Turley got sent off for the second consecutive match and we were sent packing to the tune of 4-1. Thank goodness Max got back on the coach with the lads and with luck we won't see Dover or those cliffs again – at least not in footballing terms.

BT on the other hand encountered problems of his own. Firstly there was an abusive telephone call from one of our so-called fans to his home during the game. I don't know what they thought that would achieve as Brian was obviously at the match. One guy actually tried to physically attack him but was thankfully restrained. All very distasteful, but angry fans have no sensible thoughts in their heads. However such behaviour was totally unacceptable and Brian, although obviously upset by the outburst, handled the situation admirably. The chairman continued to see the whole situation philosophically when in the 'Non-League Paper', he said, "If we've lost three on the trot, that must mean we are due for a win now, doesn't it?. I am not going to get into a panic. Why have sleepless nights about something that's already happened? Anyway this is my hobby and you have to pay for your pleasures, don't you?"

# TEN OF DIAMONDS

*B.T. issues instructions whilst Terry Westley looks on.*

"When people have a go at Brian they're actually having a go at me. I'm the creator of all this. Brian gets upset when things don't go right but he knows I support him and will continue to do so. If somebody else came in, they'd find it just as difficult. In his four seasons with us, Brian has never been out of the top four. That's not a bad record, is it? "Blame the system, not the man".

So would the tide now turn, and was Max's prediction that we were due a win prove to be correct? You bet it would and it started at Hayes on December 9th and the club never looked back. Yeovil had kept winning and established a substantial lead but there was still plenty of time left to catch them, and so it proved.

The 3-0 win at Hayes came about mainly due to some poor goalkeeping but the result was more important than the performance and the team started to believe it was up and running.

A 5-1 home win over Hednesford followed immediately but two points were dropped undeservedly at Nuneaton Borough on Boxing Day in a 1-1 draw. Now January was to be a crunch month in the bid to catch our only real rivals Yeovil Town. We had three tough league fixtures and an FA Trophy 3rd Round at Hayes to contend with and we won them all!

On January 1st, the return fixture with Nuneaton Borough was played out in a tense atmosphere at Nene Park before our 4,000 fans. How we performed on that first day of the year 2001 could make or break the rest of the season, but we managed to win 2-1 with goals from Brady and Darby.

One is always concerned about playing Southport at Haig Avenue, particularly as their current form was good. We had lost 2-1 there last season and I could think of many venues where the prospects of victory would have been far greater. They are an enigmatic side and so it proved again as the Diamonds swept to a 3-1 win. The FA Trophy gave us a little respite from our league pressures but it took another battle and another Duane Darby goal to see off Hayes 1-0 at Church Road.

# Conference Champions At Last

It was two weeks before the next game and what could be more difficult than Stevenage Borough away? But belief was back and the 2-0 win was the first time that the Diamonds had ever won at Broadhall Way. It had looked like another weekend off for the players when heavy snow fell on the Friday night to close nearby Luton Airport. However, volunteers got cracking clearing the pitch but perhaps wished they hadn't bothered as Duane Darby delivered a two-goal salvo to secure a 2-0 win.

The Diamonds were inching closer to Yeovil but the hill still looked mighty steep. Cup competitions can be a pain when one is fighting a more important league battle, but on the other hand they can also provide a timely and pleasant change of tempo, and Marine of Liverpool in the 4th round of the FA Trophy was just that.

The Merseyside club was completely overrun on a pitch that was flat rolled mud to start with and within 15 minutes resembled a ploughed field. Goals came from all over the field as the Diamonds emerged as 6-0 winners, with both substitutes Jim Rodwell and trialist Roy Essandoh scoring in the final minutes. Essandoh who was released shortly afterwards hit the limelight later in the FA Cup when scoring for Wycombe Wanderers against Leicester City after being found on the Internet by the desperate Wycombe manager.

Back to the league programme and seven points from the next three games against Forest Green Rovers (A) 0-0, Scarborough (H) 1-0, and Northwich Victoria (H) 2-1, maintained our challenge. At the end of these three matches, Diamonds had their noses in front by virtue of a better goal difference on 60 points, but Yeovil still had two games in hand!

The last Saturday in February saw a poor display in the FA Trophy 5th Round again at Forest Green Rovers. The 2-0 defeat for the Diamonds could be seen as a blessing in disguise but that wasn't quite BT's interpretation!

We were now into March and with six league matches scheduled for the month, it was Woking, a non-league colossus of the not too distant past but now a struggling side, who visited Nene Park. Duane Darby and a first for Shaun Carey got the goals in a 2-0 win but equally importantly the Diamonds secured a two point lead over Yeovil who could only draw with Stevenage Borough 1-1. However the West Country club still had those two games in hand but it was becoming decidedly tighter.

The final two minutes of the Woking game saw Mark Sale come on as substitute to a tumultuous reception. He had returned from his horrendous cancer illness with a clean bill of health, and BT's decision was welcomed by the fans.

The title race really opened up the following Saturday and although we were disappointed when a late Boston United equaliser meant that we left York Road with only a point, this was turned to joy when ex-Diamonds Dale Watkins snatched a late double for Kettering Town to defeat Yeovil.

Two points lost had suddenly become one point gained. Could the Poppies really want the Diamonds to clinch the championship?

However, three days later we would really find out with our own visit to Rockingham Road and it really was a 'must-win' situation. Local derby matches invariably produce talking point incidents and sure enough this game didn't disappoint in that way.

Justin Jackson was dramatically sent off following an adjudged dive which earned a second yellow card booking and left the Diamonds with 55 minutes to play with only ten men. Even so, the Poppies were unable to create any clear cut chances and the Duane Darby double gave Diamonds a deserved 2-0 victory and a step nearer to the title, while Kettering Town were left to ponder the ignominy of relegation – which eventually materialised,

Duane Darby scored his 20th league goal to beat Kingstonian 2-1 at Nene Park with yet another double, and sent Diamonds further ahead with the news that Yeovil had only drawn 0-0 at Morecambe. However a 0-0 draw at Northwich Victoria followed by a 1-1 home draw with Leigh RMI meant four points had gone missing and to add to the Diamonds woe, Tarkan Mustafa was sent off against Leigh and would miss the game at Hereford.

# Ten of Diamonds

There were now seven league matches still to play for the Diamonds but as the spring days grew longer so doubts over whether April would deliver the desired rewards, grew larger. It is the time of year when a whole season's efforts can disappear so easily as players get more anxious. A fifteen league match unbeaten run was still ongoing – back in December Max said, "We were due for a win". How right he was – but could we hold it together?

In football, only a few can succeed and in the Conference only one. Was it to be Yeovil or Rushden and Diamonds? We were soon to find out.

In fact, April started sensationally with a sparkling 4-1 demolition of Morecambe and Duane Darby got his first hat-trick of the season, taking his personal tally to 26 goals in just 35 games.

Dagenham & Redbridge with nine straight wins had surged up the league – some said unnoticed, but we were very much aware of them! Nevertheless it was still Yeovil who were our main challengers and a Patmore last minute winner at Kingstonian after the London side had led on three occasions kept them very much in the hunt.

Hereford has always been difficult for the Diamonds to even get a point, and although we had never won there we were confident this time with 16 unbeaten matches behind us. Any such illusions were quickly dispelled as Hereford raced into a 3-0 lead inside 37 minutes and never looked in danger of conceding more than a consolation goal midway through the second half.

Our advantage was reduced to a two point lead when over the Hereford tannoy, and to great cheering from the home fans, it was announced that Yeovil had thrashed Leigh RMI by 6-1.

The Easter holiday programme usually holds the key to any title hopes and with Doncaster Rovers at Nene Park, this game certainly fell into that category. An inspired goalkeeping display by Rovers' Barry Richardson was enough to thwart Diamonds from winning comfortably and they had to settle for a 0-0 draw in front of an anxious 4,036 fans. The position was now very clear – Diamonds led the table by three points but Yeovil had a game in hand but Diamonds held the goal difference advantage!

The 21st of April was definitely Diamonds 'D' Day. Two thousand fans made the long trek to Yeovil to urge their side on to a victory that would almost – I said almost – guarantee them the championship. A draw for Diamonds would be quite acceptable whilst a win for Yeovil was unthinkable.

As it turned out, an 8,868 crowd saw a stalemate match with Diamonds quite content with the 0-0 scoreline. Brian Talbot said, "A draw was a fair result". And so it was.

We left Yeovil quietly confident but knowing that football is so unpredictable and there could still be some more twists and turns. Three to go.

Telford at Nene Park three days after the Yeovil game saw another 4,000 plus gate and it was only in the 44th minute that Justin Jackson scored what was to be his 20th goal of the season, and eased the tension. However Jon Brady's goal 5 minutes into the second half was so important and when midfield supremo Garry Butterworth scored one of his rare goals in the 70th minute, it was all over. A 3-0 win and the goal difference advantage nicely increased!

On Saturday April 28th, Dover Athletic were the visitors to Nene Park. Back in early December when the fans wanted Brian Talbot sacked, Dover had beaten the Diamonds 4-1 and heaped humiliation on the club, the chairman and the manager. Now it was pay-back time.

5,482 fans cheered the Diamonds forward and sure enough it was Duane Darby who gave them a 17th minute lead. Dover equalised but Mark Peters headed what was to prove the winner and his first goal of the season. News that Yeovil had won at Telford brought the comment from BT: "It's going to go right down to the wire. I think Yeovil will win their last two games and I'm not expecting anything else".

The situation was crystal clear. If Yeovil won their last two home games against Hereford and Scarborough, then Rushden & Diamonds had to win at Chester which would clinch the championship on the far better goal difference.

# Conference Champions At Last

*Duane Darby celebrates after scoring against Dover.*

Yeovil's massive lead in December when they led by seven points with a game in hand had been overturned. It was now or never.

The game in hand which Yeovil still had was to be played on the Tuesday evening in the week prior to the season ending on the Saturday. If they were going to slip up at all, this would be the game against relative neighbours Hereford, because their home game on the Saturday against struggling Scarborough was an absolute banker.

The evening of the Yeovil v Hereford game, my wife and I had been invited to a special birthday party in the Seasons Bistro at the Diamond Centre for Maureen Debanke, wife of Peter. There were fourteen of us in the part which included my co-director Robert Langley, my pal and Diamonds sponsor Frank Langley (no relation) and one of our players, Jon Brady.

I had made it very clear that under no circumstances did I wish to know any interim scores, although there were others who were keeping abreast of the happenings in Somerset on their mobile telephones. At around 9.40pm, Maureen's daughter Sarah, sitting opposite me, let out a scream of sheer joy. The incredible smile on her face said it all. "Hereford have beaten Yeovil 3-2!", she screamed, "They scored the winner in the last minute!"

Pandemonium broke loose. Diners at other tables looked on in amazement. What on earth was going on? We leapt about, we shouted, we hugged and kissed. WE WERE THE CONFERENCE CHAMPIONS!!!!!!

The meal was never finished, the pudding was left untouched. Chris Smith and wife Meryl who had been watching a Junior Cup match in the stadium came running into the bistro as soon as they heard the news. They were to be the first of many delighted officials and fans who would soon descend on the club. Mark Darnell suddenly appeared having rung

# Ten of Diamonds

the chairman and raced over to join the party. Within minutes, Max arrived in the car park and as soon as he got out of the car he was hoisted shoulder high and carried down Diamond Way by fans who were arriving in their numbers. Cameramen and reporters appeared from nowhere. The Strikers bar was heaving as Max stood on a chair to make an emotional speech. In particular, he praised Brian who had come through a difficult time.

Mark managed to contact Brian who had been to Chester in preparation for Saturday's erstwhile big game but he already knew the result. He tried to persuade him to come to the club and join the celebrations but I think that he wanted to enjoy the day at Chester with his players and management team. I also don't think he had forgotten some of the fans anger only a few months earlier and I could understand his feelings.

It was simply a wonderful night at the club and we partied until 1.30am – nobody wanted to leave. We now knew that we were going to Chester in a completely relaxed frame of mind although I'm certain Brian still wanted to finish it off in style.

Chester is a beautiful city at any time but on that sunny May morning, it looked even more splendid. The main shopping centre was full of Diamonds fans as we mingled, watching the street jugglers and a guy on a high penny-farthing bike performing in what was now a very festive atmosphere.

Although we were aware it might happen, we were nonetheless surprised to come across a procession of Chester fans carrying a coffin in a gesture of anger and defiance against their chairman, American Terry Smith. This was their way of showing their desire to see him ejected from the club and illustrating how, in their eyes, he had killed off their club.

As for Chris Smith, Ted Carroll and myself, we decided that a splendid lunch was the obvious requirement before proceeding to the Deva Stadium and joining our colleagues for the final match. Despite all the traumas at their club, the Chester players responded magnificently. They lined up on the pitch to applaud the Rushden & Diamonds players, as Paul Underwood, captaining the side in the continued absence of Ray Warburton, led the team out into the sunlight. They then proceeded to bombard us and took a deserved lead soon after the interval. We consoled ourselves that it didn't really matter, but it did!

Mark Peters headed the equaliser three minutes later and with only five minutes remaining, Jon Brady took centre stage with a 30-yard speculative drive and the 2,500 fans erupted. At the final whistle a very strange thing occurred as hundreds of Diamonds fans raced onto the pitch to celebrate together with Chester supporters who stood in front of the main stand chanting for Terry Smith's head. The Chester stewards made no effort to disperse them and also sat down on the pitch in protest.

Whilst the disparity of the two sets of fans created a weird finale to the season, it did not really detract from our own enjoyment of what we had achieved.

News then came through that Yeovil had not won their last game against Scarborough but in fact had lost 1-0 – a remarkable score but one that illustrates how easy it is to fall away when the main chance has slipped away. We know – we had been there!

The Nationwide Conference rostrum was erected in the middle of the pitch and the Diamonds players filed out in twos to collect their medals. The championship and promotion to the Football League was ours and how we celebrated yet again. Instead of a goal difference win or a three points win, all of a sudden we had triumphed by a clear 6 points.

Two days later we gathered at the training centre for the commencement of our open top bus tour that would proceed to Rushden via the villages and then drive back down the A6 trunk road through Higham Ferrers, into Irthlingborough and finally to the Stadium at Nene Park.

All along the route crowds turned out in their thousands and even one daring lass on a balcony got the biggest cheer from our lads when she quickly bared her boobs!

As we approached Nene Park we could see and hear a jazz band welcoming us home. The champions had arrived!

# Conference Champions At Last

*Paul Underwood leads out the team at Chester.*

*The celebrations begin at Chester.*

*The Open Top Bus Tour.*

# Ten of Diamonds

Would you believe that 3,000 fans came to a reserve game that evening? Well not really, they had come to see the players parading and displaying the Conference championship trophy before the game started – and so we had another party!

\*      \*      \*      \*      \*      \*

Could we carry forward our momentum that had seen us lose only once in the final 22 match run-in since that eventful day at Dover? Could we make an impression in the Third Division of the Football League?

We had barely three months to find out.

*Club Captain Roy Warburton with the Conference Trophy.*

# 14
# THE FOOTBALL LEAGUE – WE'VE ARRIVED!

**IN the summer of 2001 with the beginning of the first season in the Football League beckoning, Brian Talbot took a philosophical look at the club's prospects. In an interview with Rick Broadbent, reporting for The Times, Brian said,**

"These players have spent three years getting us promoted, so it's only right I give them a chance. If after four months I have to re-evaluate, then I will, because the chairman is not going to let our league status slip. Yes, we have spent too much money in the past, but that's because people (opposing clubs) up their prices for us. They see us coming. I've got the best chairman going. He's like a father to me and he's the boss."

"I got a call from him and he said it would be fun. I said, 'Fun? Mr Chairman, managers get sacked!' He said, 'We don't sack managers here'. He offered me a contract at the end of last season but I wouldn't insult him by signing it. We just shook hands. His word is his bond. I'm under no illusions. This season will be very hard but we're not in a hurry"

Well, that's how BT saw it at that particular time. In fact, he signed two players in the summer and ironically both were from Yeovil, who had pushed us to the limit in the Conference the previous season.

They were goalkeeper Tony Pennock, who obviously fancied his chances of ousting Billy Turley and Warren Patmore, the big burly striker who BT had fancied for quite a while and who had been Yeovil's leading scorer for the past four seasons.

As it turned out, Pennock spent most of the season on the bench, except when

*Tony Pennock*

# TEN OF DIAMONDS

Turley was sent off in successive matches. He has since been sold to Farnborough Town for £25,000.

However Warren Patmore was a story and a half and he was only with us a few weeks.

After training hard in pre-season, scoring a hat-trick in a friendly against Peterborough United and a fine headed goal against a full-strength West Ham United side, all looked set for the rebirth of his football league career. He even got the nod from the manager over the previous season's leading scorer Duane Darby to start at York City, and then went one further by scoring the only goal with a spectacular back-heel flick. What a start.

Within three weeks, he asked to be released from his contract!

Prior to joining us, we were aware that Warren had a successful North London business but he had made arrangements that would allow him to go full-time – there was to be no problem – but there was!

He realised that he had been over-optimistic in resuming as a full-time player and felt he could not keep it going – or that's what he said. So with Brian Talbot's blessing, he arranged his own transfer to Woking on the basis that they had to pay us a fee equivalent to the 'signing on fee' and wages he had received from us.

*Warren Patmore and Arsenal's Tony Adams.*

So we came out of it financially OK, and Warren returned to part-time football and his business. The only down side was that we were a striker short so early in the season.

# The Football League – We've Arrived!

However before we got down to the serious stuff that awaited us in the Third Division, we had a tremendous boost when Arsenal's assistant manager Pat Rice, an old pal of BT from his Gunners days, rang asking if we could accommodate them in a friendly at Nene Park on Saturday, July 21st. He said that his boss Arsene Wenger had promised to bring his first team squad, but unfortunately we already had a friendly fixed at Boreham Wood. BT made the obvious explanations and apologies to Boreham Wood and the game with Arsenal went ahead.

Good to his word, Wenger fielded a side that was captained by Tony Adams and included the big star names of Seaman, Keown, Henry, Bergkamp and Ljunberg, to name a few.

*Arsenal striker Thierry Henry between Gary Mills and Sean Carey.*

Interestingly, only five players who eventually played in the last game at the Millennium Stadium, Cardiff, in the Division Three play off final, played in this game against Arsenal. They were Mustafa, Underwood, Peters, Butterworth and Gray.

It was a good indication of what was to transpire at Nene Park in the following weeks, when the manager realised a lot quicker than he ever thought likely, that several of his Conference winning team would not be good enough to make an impression in the Football League. But I'm jumping the gun.

So off to the beautiful city of York we went for our first ever taste of league football. It happened to be my wife's birthday that weekend so that Sharan gang was two short of its normal crew, as both Chris Smith and I travelled up by car with our wives – just like good husbands do!

# Ten of Diamonds

I would think that for our first-ever Football League match, a trip to York must rate as one of the most delightful places to visit. It is steeped in history, and although the invasion of a thousand Diamonds fans might not be of great significance to the elders of the walled city, nevertheless it was our special day. The Nene Valley folk had arrived.

In the same way that BT was unsure of what to expect on the field, my colleagues and I were similarly uncertain of our official reception. In fact we had been warned that Football League boardrooms would not be as friendly as in the Conference. As new boys with a high-profile reputation, it would be a welcome with a gritted teeth smile. We half expected the worst and got the best.

Although 'one swallow doesn't make a summer', all I can say is that the York City directors were particularly nice. Even their 88-year-old immaculate gentleman – a retired director – wanted York to win the game but the Diamonds to win the league! Better than this, the taxi driver who took us to Bootham Crescent said, "Best of luck – I hope you win".

A spectacular goal from new boy Warren Patmore was sufficient to give the Diamonds that all-important 1-0 and Sunderland striker Michael Proctor, on loan to York City, said in one of the daily newspapers,

"Rushden and Diamonds were very strong at the back and I reckon they will be hard to beat. I have a feeling that they will do well in this division"

We would soon see!

Our second league game was also going to create a little bit of history with the new ITV Digital Sport channel, televising their first ever Third Division Football League match. Being the new boys in the league, the decision-makers were obviously intrigued by us, and therefore chose our home game with Lincoln City. Little did we know that this Sports Channel, backed by Carlton and Granada, would end the season in total disarray with major financial problems. As it was, 5,000 people turned up at Nene Park, which I suppose should have been an indication that few people had bought the necessary TV dishes.

It was an entertaining game of sorts, although a goal-less draw was hardly what we or the TV company really wanted. I thought that Lincoln played very well and suggested that they would be amongst the challengers. As it happened, they only just avoided relegation!

It is perhaps interesting to remember that Lincoln City was in fact the first club ever to be relegated from the Football League into the Conference back in 1987, although they went back up the following year.

In those early days, most clubs did just that, but clubs such as Doncaster, Hereford, Scarborough, Barnet and Chester are still in the Conference without any of them as yet looking likely to break free. With two clubs now to be promoted, it will be interesting to see if that changes.

As a little side issue, Justin Jackson had been awarded 'Man of the Match' with comments in our local Evening Telegraph that "Jackson's pace will trouble Third Division defences this season". However that wasn't to prove to be the case as BT transferred him to Doncaster Rovers only a few weeks later, declaring that he wasn't up to the standard required.

Strangely, Justin, who had scored 20 goals (plus many 'assists') the previous season for us and 29 goals a season earlier for Morecambe, did not settle or take part in many games at Doncaster.

Our third game of the season proved to be one of the Diamonds best displays of the season. It is hardly possible to think of a more difficult tie than Burnley, away at Turf Moor in the Worthington Cup First Round. Their team was full of quality First Division players and they were widely tipped for promotion to the Premiership.

We had a dream start when Mark Peters headed us in front and when Tarkan Mustafa hit a magnificent 25-yard screamer we were really on a high. Burnley swarmed all over us in the latter part of the second half but we held on for a memorable 3-2 victory. This was a really big scalp to capture.

# The Football League – We've Arrived!

*Mark Peters in action.*

To be fair to Burnley, their directors were top class and showed the type of hospitality that we had unfortunately never encountered in the Conference. We had to make sure that we could emulate this friendship at Nene Park, particularly after a bad defeat such as Burnley had suffered.

Our next league opponents were Macclesfield, who had been Conference champions in the season when we looked very likely to be relegated. Moss Lane, Macclesfield, with only 1,950 fans, was hardly Turf Moor but were we becoming a little picky?

The match was played on a hot late August afternoon and was instantly forgettable. Keeper Billy Turley was the man most responsible for getting another point in a dull 0-0 draw.

Three games, and we had not been beaten, was fine, but we had scored only one goal!

On the Bank Holiday Monday, Plymouth Argyle were the visitors and in their three games, they had not won so far. Therefore hopes were reasonably high for our first league win at Nene Park in front of 4,414 fans. When Duane Darby scored twice in the first half, our hopes seemed justified but Argyle had always looked lively and scored right on half time when Jim Rodwell unfortunately headed into his own net. The game changed from that moment.

Plymouth netted twice in the second period and although we had a late flurry, the game ended 3-2 to the Argyle. It is true to say that they went on to win the league in style so perhaps it wasn't as bad a result as we thought at the time. Nevertheless, BT was already becoming doubtful about certain players and we were not yet into September. Smoke signals were on the horizon and danger lay ahead for those concerned.

# TEN OF DIAMONDS

*Stuart Gray*

It was only September 1st when we visited the rather spectacular Kassam Stadium of Oxford United and the game proved to be something of a watershed for the Diamonds, and it proved to be the last game which Justin Jackson played for the club. How quickly things can change in football.

The first half had been another stalemate with a 0-0 scoreline – then the match exploded. Referee Joe Ross first of all decided that a clash involving Jim Rodwell was worthy of a red card – an astonishing decision, but there is no redress and with only ten men, the game changed. Oxford, who, like ourselves, had never looked like scoring, suddenly sparked into life and scored three times in 17 minutes.

The game appeared over but Duane Darby scored twice in the final four minutes to cause a few flutters for the home side – but not enough. Another 3-2 defeat.

BT was not impressed, but one week later he was beside himself when another poor performance at home to Southend United saw us lose 1-0. We had now registered just 5 points from the opening 18 and the alarm bells were starting to ring.

Interestingly, Mark Lea, reporting in the local Evening Telegraph, made two remarks when he stated,

"Several shrewd signings could transform this squad into contenders for promotion play-off places. But will the Nene Park Board of Directors act quickly enough and spend the money generated by Jackson's transfer?"

# THE FOOTBALL LEAGUE – WE'VE ARRIVED!

Fair comment, Mark, and you were right because BT did make some shrewd signings and we all now know what happened thereafter. On the second point of the money from Jackson's transfer, I'm afraid that it's never quite that simple. Very rarely is the money from a transfer paid up-front and it is generally over three or even four payments. Furthermore, there is the problem of getting your money on time. Unfair perhaps, but that's the way it is, just like in any other business.

*Keeper Billy Turley in typical action with mid-season signing Andy Tillson.*

# Ten of Diamonds

*Barry Hunter*

Nonetheless, we did buy Richie Hanlon for £30,000 from Peterborough United, which might seem somewhat strange considering that we had him three years earlier and swapped him for Mequel de Souza. However, Richie looked a far more accomplished player now and BT was delighted with his form as the season eventually unfolded. Sadly in a pre-season friendly only a few weeks ago, Richie suffered a cruciate ligament injury which will put him out for the whole of the 2002-03 season.

Striker Scott Partridge from Brentford, and central defender Barry Hunter from Reading then joined us on free transfers, both released by their clubs in an attempt to lower their wage bills. The financial problems were already starting to build up and they were to get worse for all concerned.

September 11th 2001, we were due to travel to Crewe Alexandra in the 2nd Round of the Worthington Cup for a 7.45 kick off.

Every person in the country, possibly in the world, knows what happened that day. Events in New York changed so many things after those horrific acts of terrorism.

I was getting ready to join my colleagues in the Sharan and then travel up to Crewe, when I decided to put the TV on before going down to the stadium. Like so many people, I just couldn't believe what was happening, and immediately rushed down to Nene Park and into Mark Darnell's office, where he and Howard Johnstone were already looking at the television.

What we saw next was even more terrible – there, live on television, we watched dumbstruck as the second plane flew straight into the other Trade Centre building.

We made our way up the M6 motorway and talked of nothing else, and football was farthest from our minds. The directors and officials of Crewe Alexandra were amongst the kindest and friendliest of people and we were to meet with many nice people as the season progressed. Perhaps it was a day for people being nice to each other. We tried hard to concentrate on the game, but it was very difficult.

After a good even match, the scoreline was still 0-0 after 90 minutes, which was encouraging because of our struggling league form. After five minutes of extra time, Paul Underwood blasted over the bar from the penalty spot and soon afterwards Billy Turley got his marching orders for kicking the ball away and arguing. Two late Crewe goals sealed their passage into the Third Round but it really didn't seem to matter. Football came a poor second on that sad day.

A visit to Leyton Orient four days later meant meeting up with their chairman, the larger-than-life Barry Hearn, who was as welcoming as ever.

Partridge, Hunter and Hanlon all made their starting debuts and we were hopeful that we could get a win – any sort of win – but we were awful. For the second time in five days,

# The Football League – We've Arrived!

Billy Turley was sent off in conceding a penalty after 33 minutes, which put Orient two up.

Then, quite amazingly, substitute keeper Tony Pennock was guilty of fouling and giving away another penalty. Pennock saved the penalty and when it was ordered to be re-taken, he saved that as well.

Referee Andy D'Urso really got into the penalty mood and then awarded the Diamonds one from which Richie Hanlon scored. It was the only way we were ever going to score and the 2-1 defeat pushed us perilously close to the bottom of the league.

Matches were coming thick and fast and three days later Torquay visited Nene Park in another 0-0 draw match. We had now acquired 6 points from a possible 24. But our luck was about to change and who better to enjoy a slice of good fortune against but our old Conference sparring partners, Cheltenham Town.

In a tight and tense affair, Jean Michel Sigere saw a rebound cannon off him and then be fumbled into the net by their keeper. It was bad luck for Cheltenham but who gave a damn about that.

Away at Exeter on a Tuesday evening seems a ridiculous fixture to me and it looked even worse until the very last minute when Richie Hanlon headed an equaliser for a 1-1 draw. By this time, Andrew Sambrook, a young right full back who just turned up at the beginning of the season and asked for a trial, had now replaced the injured Tarkan Mustafa and was to hold his place until well into the New Year.

We achieved our fourth scoreless draw at Darlington. The Quakers were one of the pre-season favourites with Chairman George Reynolds, spending an ever bigger fortune than Max on his ultra-modern 25,000 seater stadium. It wasn't ready for our visit but viewing it from the coach, it certainly looked quite magnificent. That's some stadium, George – I only hope you can half fill it!

Youth team striker Robert Duffy made his debut against a side who had scored 9 goals in their 3 previous home games and with Duane Darby still on the injured sidelines, it was a promising start for the lad

An own goal and a Barry Hunter header were enough to secure three points on a Friday night fixture at home to Hartlepool by 2-1. Our ex-striker Colin West, who was now coach at Hartlepool, returned to the North East with nothing to show for their efforts, but it was evident that they were a quality side and so it proved as the season unfolded.

Ex-Cobbler Christian Lee was on loan from Farnborough Town but made his one and only League start in that game. Another young loanee was 18 year old Caleb Folan, a tall Leeds United striker, and he made fleeting appearances before returning north to Elland Road.

Although so many changes in personnel could be unsettling, BT just had to keep trying new players, and he did. Incredibly, yet another 0-0 draw followed – it was our fifth, but considering it was away to Rochdale who were amongst the early pace-setters, I suppose it was a reasonable result. In the LDV Vans Trophy 1st Round, we took an experimental side to South Wales and got badly clobbered 7-1 by a rampant Cardiff City. Best forgotten, soonest mended!

But where and when were the goals to come from?

However another signing in the form of Paul Hall was a big plus and as the season unfolded he just got better all the time. The 29 year old Jamaican International had been signed from Walsall on a free transfer which I found absolutely staggering. BT in the Evening Telegraph said, "He's quick and strong, although he doesn't score a lot of goals". Wrong there, Brian!

Around that particular time it also looked that Michael McElhatton might be on his way back and although he played intermittently he eventually had to face yet another operation on his knee. Subsequently he has now been told by a specialist that he will no longer be able to play at all, and the Macca revival has unfortunately had a very sad ending indeed.

# Ten of Diamonds

Duane Darby who had missed eight consecutive matches, returned for the big game at Nene Park against title favourites, big spending Hull City. A tremendous game in which Hull fought back from 3-1 down at the interval to level the scores, got everyone buzzing again. Andy Burgess scored twice (his first goals of the season), with Richie Hanlon netting the other goal and confirming his ability to get goals from the midfield region.

The following Tuesday we visited the lovely town of Shrewsbury and after a quick reconnaissance it was down to the serious business of getting maximum points. We were putting together a run of undefeated matches but wins were scarce – but not on that particular evening. Setchell and Darby scored in each half but with Hanlon and Hunter well bedded in and with Hall's pacy forays, the whole side looked capable of better things.

*Andy Burgess leaps in delight at his goal.*

Mansfield Town at Nene Park were our next opponents, another side who were promising to be distinct promotion possibilities. However their main goalscorer, Greenacre, was missing and we simply had to capitalise on this. They looked a lively outfit and scored first, but once they conceded an own goal, Burgess and Partridge wrapped up the points with a 3-1 win. Unbeaten in nine!

Swansea at Vetch Field can be a daunting place to visit at any time but on this particular occasion it took on a somewhat more sinister feel. From the time we set foot in the stadium, we encountered the home fans' anger – not at us, but at their new owner and chairman Tony Petty. "We want Petty out!" will forever be ingrained in my mind. From the moment Tony Petty emerged into the director's box and calmly sat himself down to watch the first ever match between Swansea and the Diamonds, he was a marked man. Well actually a marked man is hardly the correct description. Abused, violated, reviled and insulted are just a few adjectives which might come close to describing the 90 minutes which he endured.

# The Football League – We've Arrived!

He had been warned that a demonstration was on the cards, but this was really nasty and sustained. The visiting Director's Box was right in the line of fire and the hatred was truly incredible. Meanwhile, Mr Petty sat totally unmoved throughout. It really was an amazing stoic performance on his part. Apparently Tony Petty had only taken over Swansea City FC five weeks earlier.

Although it had cost him nothing in immediate financial terms, he nevertheless would ultimately be responsible for their ever increasing debts and £700,000 for this season was now anticipated. What he did was to address the problem and thereby incense the fans.

Two seasons ago Swansea had been promoted, and on the back of that success, a whole batch of new inflated contracts had been given to the players. The team stuttered badly, relegation followed but obviously the players' contracts remained. The big salaried players were told that wages would be slashed and/or they could seek employment with another club with immediate effect. The whole squad was up for sale!

Certainly dramatic measures were required because someone had to pay the bills. Obviously I don't know the full facts but I do know I will always remember our visit to Vetch Field for the wrong reasons. Even when we left the ground some 45 minutes after the game, the streets were awash with irate fans (some as young as seven or eight years), stewards and police – a sad sight indeed.

Soon afterwards Mr Petty left the club and I've no idea what became of him or the actual outcome of what he left behind. However I do know that the 90 minutes of a sterile 0-0 draw will be forever remembered for the protests rather than the game.

Trialists continued to enter our Training Complex with such regularity that it was hard to keep track. Peter Thompson from Luton Town was another who was no longer required by the Hatters so BT, always hoping that a goalscorer might emerge literally out of a hat, took him on loan.

In fact against Halifax, Thompson came on as a second half substitute and scored, together with Scott Partridge to ensure three points and a 2-1 win at Nene Park. Now that Football League status had been achieved it meant that we did not have to play in the Fourth Qualifying Round of the FA Cup, but the 1st round tie, away to Worcester City from the Dr Martens Southern League. Premier Division was not what we wanted, one little bit.

The expected tough cup tie certainly materialised and only a stunning 30 yard free kick from Richie Hanlon in the 65th minute separated the teams. But we were through to the second round and desperately looked forward to a home tie, but no such luck! In the meantime, another league match was upon us three days later with Scunthorpe coming to town – well, Irthlingborough, actually!

They had visited us before in the FA Cup when as a non-league side we had beaten them 2-0 in fine style – but this game was quite different. Peter Beagrie, an ex-Premiership star and crowd pleaser, was something of a gamble for Scunthorpe in their quest for Division Two status. He certainly showed his class but the match drifted into yet another 0-0 draw – our seventh of the season!

Kidderminster Harriers away was probably our worst performance in the league to date. We were badly beaten 3-0 and were second best in all departments with our old Conference buddies taking great delight in their superiority. However watching from the stand was another Jamaican International by the name of Onandi Lowe and he could not have been impressed by what he had seen.

The 27 year old 6 foot 4" striker who had made over 50 appearances for Jamaica had played half a game in the reserves during the week and although not fit, had BT hopping with anticipation.

However would he be interested in coming to us on loan for three months from Kansas City Wizards and could we do a deal with the American Major Soccer League to whom he was contracted?

# Ten of Diamonds

*B.T. with Onandi Lowe.*

On the one hand, Brian really fancied him but reports from Port Vale where he had tried his luck in the previous season were not complimentary. Nonetheless, BT decided to take the plunge. Protracted negotiations across the Atlantic, both with the USA and Jamaica eventually resulted in an agreement and Onandi joined us on the maximum 3 month loan period. When the three months were up we then had to sign him on contract or he would simply return to the States.

It was not ideal but it gave us breathing space. On Decmber 3rd, Onandi Lowe made his debut at Nene Park against Bristol Rovers before 4,570 fans and gave everyone a taste of what was to follow. Scott Partridge scored in the first minute, then Onandi Lowe scored with the first of his many thunderbolts, followed by another Partridge goal to seal a 3-1 win.

The hoped-for FA Cup home tie did not happen – yet another away draw this time at Brighton and Hove Albion who had only been promoted to the second division the previous season and were now flying high with aspirations of yet another elevation to the 1st Division. However there was considerable concern about their temporary home at the Withdean Athletic Stadium being acceptable in the short term, should they get promotion again. They needed a 10,000 capacity stadium for Division One but were hoping for a Football League moratorium which would enable them to be promoted. As it eventually happened, Brighton were promoted but must now come good with a new stadium and within a given time scale.

Brighton, with their star young striker Bobby Zamora scoring yet again, just about deserved the 2-1 win on the day.

I would like to think that one day in the FA Cup we might get drawn against Manchester United or Arsenal – dreams, maybe. But this club has been built on dreams!

The week before Christmas, we made the short trip to Luton Town who together with Plymouth Argyle were already looking good promotion bets. Duane Darby was back from injury and partnered Onandi Lowe but the Hatters rear guard held the upper hand and just one goal was enough for them to claim all three points. A draw would probably have been a fairer result but you don't always get what's fair.

Christmas Eve – forget about last minute shopping and come to Nene Park was the message. 4,142 did just that for the visit of Carlisle United. A Paul Hall inspired victory with Onandi netting again saw us home by 3-1. It was our ninth consecutive home game without defeat.

Exactly 12 months earlier a section of the fans had been calling for BT's head and now here we were in 8th spot in the 3rd Division only one place from the play offs!

However just to prove that nothing can be taken for granted in this game, we visited Roots Hall on Boxing Day and Southend United completed the double over us winning 4-2 after being 2-0 down at half time. A major casualty and not through injury was Jim Rodwell,

# The Football League – We've Arrived!

a solid central defender who had performed with great distinction for the club. After the Southend game Jim never played again for the first team.

Even the following Saturday when the team had the long trek to league leaders Plymouth Argyle, Jim was omitted and Paul Underwood took his place at the centre of defence with the ever reliable Gary Setchell in at left back. It was a sad and abrupt end to Jim's time at Nene Park as he had been a very likeable lad, but BT was determined to tighten up in all areas and Barry Hunter would soon be back alongside Mark Peters.

Plymouth in the last playing day of 2001 was a hard call, particularly as in midfield we had both Stuart Gray and Macca in the team after lengthy injuries. It was a bridge too far but a 1-0 defeat at the splendidly refurbished Home Park against the champions elect was not the worst way to end the year.

The chairman went on record at that time stating, "I feel for the first time in nine years that I'm not under pressure to win the league. I think it's wonderful in the 3rd Division and I'm enjoying every minute of it. This time last year our championship ambitions looked over but we lost just one game between the New Year and early May – so I know anything is possible, even this season!"

Prophetic words, Max.

Quite similarly to the previous season we had suffered five consecutive away defeats at this stage and this needed rectifying the sooner the better. And it certainly got better as soon as the New Year kicked off.

The Diamonds returned from Sincil Bank, Lincoln, with three points after a very action packed encounter, winnng 4-2. Again, Lowe had set the ball rolling after only four minutes and then Paul Hall twice and Duane Darby completed the scoring. BT insisted, "We are going to attack teams and take games by the scruff of the neck". Game on!

York City perished 3-0 at Nene Park and fans on the Peter Debanke Terrace saw two of their favourite sons – Duane Darby and Macca score right in front of them. Onandi added a late third and everything in the camp looked decidedly rosy, until……….

We were faced with two separate horror journeys to the North West and then the North East in the same week. Daunting enough in itself but injuries had quickly piled up and club skipper Ray Warburton who had hitherto not played all season was persuaded to step into the breach. With Darby and Macca still only 80% fit and Lowe and Underwood left behind on the physio's treatment table, the result of 3-0 to Carlisle told its story, except that the score against us could easily have been doubled. The 5-1 defeat by Hartlepool only highlighted our problems with Wardley, Douglas and Carr, all new loan players, never having previously met up with the other players. It showed, and Darren Carr didn't even finish the match with Youth Team player John Dempster replacing him for his first outing with the senior squad. Another Youth player, striker Robert Duffy, came on late in the game and scored our only goal with a fine header.

There were two redeeming features of our first ever visit to Hartlepool. One was the emergence of a couple of youngsters who did enough to suggest they could well 'come through the system', and secondly, the incredible friendliness of the officials at the Hartlepool club. Top marks!

We had now lost seven of the last eight away matches and were glad to be back on home soil for Macclesfield's visit on the Tuesday evening of the following week. Stuart Wardley scored on his home debut and Onandi Lowe added the second in a 2-0 win.

It was Darlington's turn to come to Nene Park on the next Saturday and our good home form continued with the two reggae boys Paul Hall and Onandi Lowe on target in a 2-1 win.

The third consecutive home game in 10 days saw Oxford United, now under the management of ex-Cobblers boss Ian Atkins, arrive at Nene Park and go under the hammer 2-1 in a very tight match. After Lowe had opened our scoring, and the visitors had equalised, substitute Jon Brady scored a sensational winner with a trademark free kick with only ten

# Ten of Diamonds

minutes remaining. His leap onto the railings of the North Stand to greet his brother who had just arrived from Australia said it all.

BT was as cautious as ever, having just picked up 9 points from three games in just over a week as his comments showed. He said, "I think we are mathematically safe now – 48 points will be enough. I don't think Halifax will get 48 points. However I don't know whether we will finish in the top seven, but we think we've got a chance"

However after the game, Barry Hunter was confirmed as having broken a bone in his foot and would be out for quite a while, so Brian moved quickly by signing Andy Tillson on a free transfer, again from Walsall. It seemed mighty strange to me that Walsall had allowed us two tremendous free transfers in Hall and Tillson but such are the vagaries of football.

Although Tillson immediately fitted into the side like a hand in a glove, his first three games saw us stutter a little. A 2-1 defeat at Hull was followed by a 1-1 home draw against Rochdale and a fortuitous 1-0 home win over Leyton Orient meant four points from nine. The good news that Onandi Lowe had signed a 2 year contract and would therefore be available for the remainder of our season's push for the play offs was greeted with renewed hope. In typical Caribbean style, Onandi said, "I feel at home and relaxed, so we can start from here and let it flow" – whatever that meant!

Before the fixtures for the season came out, Torquay was earmarked as a good overnight step for the Sharan gang. We could meander along the seafront looking at the boats and enjoy the warmth of the so-called English Riviera. Not if you are destined to visit in February and it's bucketing down with torrential rain!

Stuart Wardley had given us a first half lead but Andrew Sambrook unfortunately sliced a low cross into his own net to give Torquay a deserved equaliser. Although they

*"Can this really be Torquay?"*

were languishing near the bottom of the league it again proved that there were no easy matches.

The first Saturday in March saw us visit Cheltenham Town who were already looking like automatic promotion contenders. I had made up my mind that I was going to try and tackle a festering sore that I felt had developed between the two clubs from way back in our Conference days together.

It was well known that BT and their manager Steve Cotterill were not the best of mates but I felt that relations at director level should be more amenable – I said so. The directors I spoke to seemed surprised at my comments but after making my point, I felt that we might all get on rather better in the future.

As for the game, it will be remembered for a wonder goal from Onandi Lowe to cancel out Julian Alsop's earlier header. It really was something special but we were becoming accustomed to this sort of thing from the boy from Jamaica.

142

# The Football League – We've Arrived!

Another crazy evening fixture meant Exeter had to return the compliment and travel half the length of the country for a Tuesday night game. BT bought back Mustafa and Hanlon to increase the attacking options and a 2-1 win justified the move with a Burgess goal and Hanlon penalty. We had now extended our unbeaten home run to 16 games.

On Saturday March 9th nearly 6,000 fans poured into Nene Park for what is our nearest thing to a local derby, against Luton Town, who now looked certain as runners up or even still possibly champions. Those two fixtures against Exeter in midweek and Luton on the Saturday just highlights the nonsense of fixture making.

In a tight game, Diamonds took an early second half lead through Paul Hall but the Hatters stormed back and showed why they are a top team by snatching a 2-1 win. Thus ended our unbeaten home record.

I didn't see the next four games because I was away in Spain with friends, but did we enjoy the scorelines as they came through on the telly! First it was Bristol Rovers. A name that had been synonymous with football seemingly since eternity. Having been relegated from the 2nd Division only the previous season, they were now struggling near the bottom of the third. Famous name or not, there is little sentiment in business or in football. I was later told that they were quite poor and the Diamonds 3-0 victory at the Memorial Stadium could easily have been doubled. Onandi Lowe and Richie Hanlon netted the goals that sent my friends, my wife and I out to dinner on the Saturday evening in really good heart. The Rioja always tastes better after a good win.

When you are abroad and well away from the action, there is a tendency (certainly in my case) of checking everything down to the finest of details. The top ten teams were now being closely monitored and the league tables carefully scrutinised right down to goal difference.

With play off wannabees Shrewsbury Town the next visitors to Nene Park, us guys in Spain were now waiting on every word and TV scoreline to tell the best or the worst of the happenings back home. As we sat waiting for the score to come up on the telly, we didn't know that 5,432 fans had roared the Diamonds on to a 3-0 victory.

I saw the game a couple of weeks later on video and it wasn't as one-sided as the score suggests, but it was 3 more points and also 3 more goals! Lowe, Hanlon and Mustafa did the business in the goal department.

The following Saturday was a really big one, as if they weren't all big ones at this time of the year. Before ever being involved in a league where the play-offs were involved, I wasn't too thrilled at the idea of a team finishing seventh getting promoted over a team that had achieved fourth spot. Not now, oh, definitely not now!!

So away to Mansfield Town, currently third in the table, at their Field Mill ground was obviously going to be a very difficult task. Not a bit of it. Of the 5,800 fans inside the ground at the start, apparently there was a thousand less at the finish.

Onandi Lowe had smashed a hat-trick by the 63rd minute in a tremendous 4-1 win and the disgruntled home fans were streaming out well before the final whistle. Brett Angell, a widely travelled and experienced campaigner had been signed as cover on loan in case of an injury to Lowe, but it was his partner Darby who was carried off and Angell netted the fourth goal after coming on as a first half substitute.

Earlier in the day I had said that if we could win at Mansfield (which I didn't think we really could), then a bottle of our own best champagne would be opened to celebrate. I could hardly believe the 4-1 scoreline – this was fantastic – three consecutive wins and the bubbly tasted wonderful!

We only had to wait two more days until the Bank Holiday Monday – April 1st, when Swansea City came to town. Onandi Lowe who netted two more goals was somewhat aggrieved to be substituted with 20 minutes remaining, but BT was certainly protecting his ace card, and with Hall and Angell also scoring the 4-0 scoreline sounded very sweet.

# Ten of Diamonds

By now, we were dining out in style. The standard of restaurants took an upward turn on the strength of four victories, 12 points and 14 goals scored, with a massive 13 goal difference!

I was back in the UK for the next game at Scunthorpe and yet again it was a battle both needed to win to secure a top seven spot. Neither did, and 1-1 was about right. After Paul Underwood sliced a header into his own net, Mr Lowe equalised with a trademark left footer with twelve minutes remaining. On the downside, 9-goal midfielder Richie Hanlon limped out of the match with a hamstring injury and it was confirmed that he wouldn't take part in any of the remaining games. If only that had been his sole injury concern!

The last two away games at Kidderminster; this season in the Football League and the previous time in the Conference must rate as possibly the worst of our performances in recent seasons.

However with only two games remaining to complete our league programme, and just one win needed to ensure a play-off semi-final spot, this game at Nene Park would lay the 'Kiddy' ghost once and for all.

5,500 expectant fans were there to witness a great achievement, but it didn't happen. We had enough chances to win comfortably but somehow we missed them all. On the other hand Kidderminster seized on two dreadful defensive errors and went home with a 2-0 win. BT summing up said, "One game doesn't make a season. You've got to be judged on 46 games and we will find out next Saturday where we finish". We sure would, Brian!

On the 20th April we set off for Halifax where we had to win.

Halifax Town had already been relegated into the Conference and it could be argued that they had nothing to play for. Added to that, the club was in turmoil with bankruptcy looming and their entire future in the balance. Five years earlier, Halifax had beaten us to the Conference championship and promotion into the Football League – now we were fighting for the right to fight out a four team battle to gain promotion to the 2nd division!

A dubious penalty put Halifax ahead after 21 minutes and the score remained 1-0 until the interval. Then Onandi took centre stage. He headed two fine goals in the opening five minutes after the resumption and then Wardley and Hall made the game safe. A late Halifax goal was of no consequence and the 4-2 win was again indicative of our ability to score goals regularly.

Unfortunately Andy Burgess had been sent off for retaliation which meant he could take part in the Play-Off semi-finals but not in the final at Cardiff, should we make it.

In our first season in the Football League 3rd Division, Rushden & Diamonds had secured 6th position – a fine achievement. Plymouth Argyle were champions, Luton Town were runners-up and Mansfield Town were the third team who would automatically be promoted.

Cheltenham Town who had looked almost certain to get an automatic promotion place had faltered in the final run-in and finished in 4th place. Rochdale were 5th, Rushden & Diamonds 6th, with Hartlepool having come with a late run to snatch 7th spot ahead of Shrewsbury and Scunthorpe. Hull City who had been the choice of many as championship favourites had fallen away very badly and finished in 11th position.

It was now or never time.

Excitement at Nene Park in the week building up to our home leg against Rochdale was immense. Both our League encounters had ended in draws, 0-0 and 1-1 so there was very little to choose between the sides and so it proved yet again.

6,000 fans roared their teams on from the outset and it was only seven minutes before McEvilly set the Rochdale contingent alight with a spectacular solo goal. On the half hour Wardley found space and headed home for the equaliser. The game ebbed and flowed at tremendous pace with both keepers in constant action. Was this really a 3rd division semi-final?

Eleven minutes into the second half, Simpson's spectacular 35 yarder whistled past Turley before he could hardly move and Rochdale were in front again. Onandi Lowe twice had goals disallowed for reasons not clear to us spectators but then Diamonds longest serving player,

# The Football League – We've Arrived!

*Garry Butterworth equalises against Rochdale in the play-off, first leg game.*

*Billy Turley saves magnificently against Rochdale in the earlier League encounter.*

# Ten of Diamonds

Garry Butterworth, smashed a right footer – I'll say it again, a right footer – from 25 yards into the top corner of the net to bring the scores level yet again at 2-2, and that's how it finished. It was a level of excitement that would be hard to follow at Rochdale in the second leg three days later – that was to be a complete understatement!

Rochdale directors and players must have travelled home to Lancashire feeling quietly confident that the hard part had been achieved but manager John Hollins, an old Arsenal team-mate of Brian's was not so sure. For our part, we were similarly confident. The pressure was now transferred to the home side. They would be expected to win, but our away form in recent weeks had been good and we had real pace up front, and we had Onandi.

Our hospitality of three days earlier was about to be reciprocated in true Lancastrian style. Inside their boardroom we were treated royally. Champagne before the game? Had someone opened the bottles a little early by mistake? Frivolity, bonhomie and graciousness was in abundance! Even the five lovely sponsorship girls that they paraded before us in the skimpiest attire managed to keep our minds occupied for a few minutes longer until kick-off time.

The real business was now at hand. Spotland was on fire, 8,485 fans expectant.

The pitch was poor. No wonder John Hollins had jokingly (I think) said after the game at Nene Park that he would be much happier to play the 2nd leg on the same pitch. Rochdale Hornets had certainly left their mark on the Spotland surface but it would be the same for both sets of players.

From the outset the Diamonds were the better side and apart from one early chance for young Townson, it seemed that only one team was going to win. But football doesn't quite work like that, but we were reasonably satisfied with the goal-less first half, and felt the second period would be kinder.

Then it happened – the howler of howlers!

Back in October, goalkeeper Billy Turley had worked miracles in getting us a 0-0 draw at Rochdale, but now the nightmare moment that keepers trougout the world must dread – happened.

A routine back pass from Mark Peters hit a divot at the very moment of Billy's kicking contact and in horror we all watched as the ball slid past him covering some dozen yards before entering the middle of the goal. I well remember turning to see the Sponsors lounge directly behind us, alive with glee. The tremendous joy of being gifted a goal out of nothing and totally against the run of play.

Even so, the 1,500 Diamonds fans continued to sing and out-shout their Dale supporters. Why don't they cheer as loud and incessantly at Nene Park?

Within two minutes, we were level and who better to score that precious equaliser than Onandi Lowe. I turned again to their Sponsors lounge but they now were looking decidedly glum. How two minutes can change the faces of football fans.

Then Onandi slid a peach of a pass to his Jamaican compatriot and Paul Hall finished in style. Who was singing now?

In the last minute of the game there must have been the longest goal mouth scramble ever – shot blocked, shot blocked again, players pushing, tumbling over, another shot blocked. Rochdale simply had to score but what seemed like an age ended when Billy Turley collected the loose ball as it came out of the scrum and fell to the ground with the biggest smile possible on his face. Then the final whistle sounded – we really were going to Cardiff!

In all my years in football the night at Rochdale has not been surpassed. The night we won the Conference without kicking a ball; the night some 30 years earlier, when Irthlingborough Diamonds won their first UCL Championship, the wonderful night at Elland Road are equals – but could not be any better. How can anything be richer than the ultimate. Back at the hotel it was glorious bedlam. We talked and talked – every incident was analysed then analysed again.

## The Football League – We've Arrived!

Who gets tired when the adrenaline is in full flow? Sleep was never going to come easy on such a wonderful night but at 3.00am I gave it best, went to bed and relived every moment over and over again.

These are the moments of footballing fantasy. What all us football lovers dream of, but rarely achieve. Rochdale have strived for decades to climb the football ladder and we were having that opportunity in a one-off final after just 12 months!

The next morning realisation came a calling – in the sober light of day we asked each other – did it really happen?

In six days time we would be heading for the Millennium Stadium in Cardiff, just ten years after the birth of our club – now on the verge of Division 2. In the following days, building up to the Bank Holiday Monday, May 6th, emotions were still running high and it must be difficult for people not connected with football to understand or appreciate the passion and excitement that this old game can generate.

\*         \*         \*         \*         \*         \*

We travelled to Cardiff on the Sunday on a coach for directors, officials, wives and special friends. Everything and everybody was so calm, it was quite strange.

The Vale of Glamorgan Hotel and Country Club was our base, and it was the hotel where only the day before Arsenal had stayed and emerged as FA Cup winners. If that was a plus omen, then the news that we had drawn the short straw of the South "Hoodoo" dressing room, from which all ten previous finalists had lost, certainly was not!

The lads had a Sunday afternoon walkabout at the Millennium Stadium and talked of little else. That evening, we dined, we laughed and we kept telling each other that it didn't really matter whether we won or lost. Well, that's what we said!

*Paul Underwood and Garry Butterworth look on in awe at the Millenium Stadium.*

# Ten of Diamonds

The morning of the match, I watched golfers teeing off on the hotel course – anything to pass the time. A few of our lads were also on the putting green trying to allay any nerves. We knew that Cheltenham had sold twice as many tickets as us, but who cared. We were now raring to go and in 30 minutes would be in the city of Cardiff.

The Millennium Stadium is very, very special and is a true football arena. Shame on the mandarins of the Football Association who cannot decide where and what to build as England's National stadium.

The Nationwide Football League luncheon for both clubs set the tone but the sheer wonder of the stadium itself as we walked into its vastness was a memory to behold. We were shown to our seats – but there must be a mistake – we were right at the front of the Royal Box – now we knew we really had arrived!

*Onandi Lowe enjoying the stadium.*

The singing, the friendly rivalry and the huge video screens all had to be soaked up in this wonderful pre-match atmosphere. I thought of my father. I remembered the boys washing in the tin bath back in 1947 and as I came back to reality I knew that possibly we were 90 minutes, 120 minutes or even a penalty shoot out away from the 2nd division.

Our recent good form and Cheltenham Town's patchy end of season hiccups, gave us heart. They had overcome Hartlepool in their two legged semi-final somewhat fortunately but we were again face to face with our old Conference counterparts.

The match itself went so quickly but from the outset I was a little disturbed at the manner in which they were stretching us. This wasn't in my script and I bet is wasn't in BT's either. Although their opening goal was rather fortuitous, it had nevertheless looked likely. As at

# The Football League – We've Arrived!

*Paul Hall – scorer of unquestionably the finest goal at the Millenium Stadium to date.*

# Ten of Diamonds

Rochdale, so at Cardiff – we hit back immediately and the equaliser was a goal all football fans dream about. It is not exaggerating to say that the Millennium Stadium in years to come is unlikely to see a goal better than that of Paul Hall's.

A mazy, pacy run from the half way line right through the centre and heart of their defence ended so magnificently with a delicate flick over the astonished keeper. It was an individual goal of sheer brilliance.

Half time at 1-1 meant we were well in the game. However the second half belonged to Cheltenham until the last few minutes when in a flurry of attacking we might easily have scored twice. As it was, a goal three minutes into the second half was soft but vital. For the next half hour we were on the back foot and when substitute Grayson smashed a shot against the post, Finnigan was handily placed to crack home the rebound. Disappointingly we had not done ourselves justice in the second half, but Cheltenham Town were worthy winners. As for the result and thereby promotion to Division 2, there were different schools of thought.

Of course we wanted to win and the thrill of a new challenge would have been exhilarating but was it all too soon? Just 12 months ago we were still in the Conference.

The collapse of the ITV Digital channel and general financial constraints could have severely tested us – maybe it was for the best.

One thing is for certain, and that is nothing can ever take away the memories of such a wonderful campaign and the glorious occasion of playing a final in the Millennium Stadium in Cardiff.

# 15
# MAX GRIGGS, C.B.E

**VIRTUALLY everyone at Rushden and Diamonds Football Club calls him Max – well, not quite everyone, because Brian Talbot from day one called him Mr Chairman as a sign of respect for the man. Subsequently Brian's management and coaching staff followed his lead, but to everyone else in football circles, he is simply Max. So who is Max Griggs – this man of the people, owner of the Dr. Martens footwear, R. Griggs and Company, but very importantly, the Chairman of Rushden and Diamonds Football Club?**

To people throughout the shoe industry and the football arena, he is Mr Nice Guy – a real gentle gentleman.

Max was born in the small Northamptonshire town of Raunds in 1938. He was an only child; the son of Bill Griggs, who was himself well known throughout the English footwear trade, who had taken over the mantle from his father, who had started the business.

Max recalls how, at ten years of age, he was sent off to a boarding school at Chicheley Hall, near Newport Pagnell, for three years. He reflects on the tough discipline imposed at the school of cold linoleum floors, iron bedsteads and the army-style inspections.

"It was hard", he once told me. "I felt alone and didn't like it at all".

He also went to the local Rushden Boot & Shoe Technical College, where he claims with pride that he was able to make a pair of shoes from scratch by the time he was fourteen years of age.

After working for a year in every department of the family business at Wollaston, Max then had a year at the Northampton College of Technology, again studying the footwear industry. He then served two years National Service, and soon afterwards met his wife-to-be, Barbara, and they were married in June 1960. He was 22 years old.

In 1961, his grandfather died and two years later Max was made a director of the company. By this time, his father had already acquired the rights of the German footwear sole soon to be named 'Airwair', and the 'Doc Martens' range came into being. It revolutionised their business and by the time that Max's father died in 1980, aged only 67, the company was making giant strides on the world footwear scene.

Max subsequently acquired the shareholding of his cousin Peter in 1989, and with his own son Stephen becoming an active participant in the company, the rate of growth continued rapidly.

As with everything in life, nothing is forever. Circumstances, markets and fashions always change. From over 200,000 pairs per week at the height of their fame, the sales of the Dr. Martens range of footwear has diminished to half of that figure. Drastic measures have followed with large scale redundancies and factory closures, but Max feels that they have an excellent chance now of a good recovery.

I recently asked Max if he had regrets on spending a fortune creating Rushden and Diamonds. His reply was emphatic.

# Ten of Diamonds

"No regrets whatsoever. I have had ten wonderful years of enjoyment and not many football Chairmen can say that. Now that we have reached our goal of being in the Football League – I just love it".

However at the moment it is seriously difficult on the business front. Considerable losses in recent years have meant that the football club must now start to stand on its own feet. The big money signings are at the moment a thing of the past, although there is no doubt that some of the biggest transfer fees paid out for goalscorers did have the desired effects and came within a whisker of the club reaching Division Two of the Football League.

His earlier foray into the world of football saw Max start watching Northampton Town back in 1961 and in 1979 he became a director, but five years later he resigned when the fans and a local reporter were calling for the directors' heads.

That was why he was very dubious about coming back into football, particularly at a lowly non-league level.

On the subject of the two managers who have performed so well over the ten years, Max is unequivocal.

"Roger Ashby set us on the way to success – he did a super job".

Nonetheless, the change of manager when it came was considered as the right decision at the right time. As regards to the present manager, Brian Talbot, he admires the way he has handled himself in difficult circumstances.

"I think the knocks he took before he joined us gave him a good insight into football's nastier side and we have got the best out of him because of that. He has done us proud".

I asked Max whether he thought his son Stephen would carry on his work at Rushden and Diamonds. Max replied:

"At the moment Stephen is quite content for me to front everything, but I am confident that cometh the time he would carry things on at Nene Park in the same way".

Hopefully that time is a long way off.

Meanwhile it is Max Griggs to whom the plaudits belong. His magnificent contribution in providing the finance – around £20 million – to build such splendid facilities in the oasis of rural Northamptonshire is simply incredible.

Max, everyone associated with the club is indebted to you, and perhaps therefore it would be fair to suggest to you that your 'Diamonds really are forever'.

# Max Griggs C.B.E.

*Max and Stephen Griggs on the balcony of the Training Centre.*

\*　　　\*　　　\*　　　\*　　　\*　　　\*

**Max Griggs was awarded the C.B.E for Services to the British Footwear Industry in January 1996, and was also awarded an Honorary M.A from the Northampton Nene University College for Services to the Local Community.**

\*　　　\*　　　\*　　　\*　　　\*　　　\*

# League Tables

## SOUTHERN LEAGUE MIDLAND DIVISION 1992-1993

| | | P | W | D | L | F | A | W | D | L | F | A | PTS |
|---|---|---|---|---|---|---|---|---|---|---|---|---|---|
| 1 | Nuneaton Borough | 42 | 12 | 4 | 5 | 53 | 23 | 17 | 1 | 3 | 49 | 22 | 92 |
| 2 | Gresley Rovers | 42 | 15 | 1 | 5 | 49 | 28 | 12 | 5 | 4 | 45 | 27 | 87 |
| 3 | Rushden & Diamonds | 42 | 15 | 4 | 2 | 51 | 17 | 10 | 6 | 5 | 34 | 24 | 85 |
| 4 | Barri | 42 | 13 | 1 | 7 | 40 | 25 | 13 | 4 | 4 | 42 | 24 | 83 |
| 5 | Newport AFC | 42 | 11 | 4 | 6 | 34 | 27 | 12 | 4 | 5 | 39 | 31 | 77 |
| 6 | Bedworth United | 42 | 10 | 4 | 7 | 31 | 29 | 12 | 4 | 5 | 41 | 26 | 74 |
| 7 | Stourbridge | 42 | 10 | 5 | 6 | 45 | 35 | 7 | 4 | 10 | 48 | 44 | 60 |
| 8 | Sutton Coldfield Town | 42 | 12 | 2 | 7 | 46 | 36 | 5 | 7 | 9 | 36 | 42 | 60 |
| 9 | Redditch United | 42 | 9 | 3 | 9 | 42 | 39 | 9 | 3 | 9 | 33 | 40 | 60 |
| 10 | Tamworth | 42 | 10 | 5 | 6 | 40 | 24 | 6 | 6 | 9 | 25 | 27 | 59 |
| 11 | Weston Super Mare | 42 | 11 | 4 | 6 | 54 | 40 | 6 | 3 | 12 | 25 | 46 | 58 |
| 12 | Leicester United | 42 | 11 | 4 | 6 | 41 | 26 | 5 | 5 | 11 | 26 | 41 | 57 |
| 13 | Grantham Town | 42 | 10 | 4 | 7 | 35 | 32 | 6 | 5 | 10 | 25 | 41 | 57 |
| 14 | Bilston Town | 42 | 11 | 5 | 5 | 47 | 30 | 4 | 5 | 12 | 27 | 39 | 55 |
| 15 | Evesham United | 42 | 5 | 7 | 9 | 36 | 41 | 10 | 1 | 10 | 31 | 42 | 53 |
| 16 | Bridgnorth Town | 42 | 7 | 6 | 8 | 28 | 31 | 8 | 1 | 12 | 33 | 37 | 52 |
| 17 | Dudley Town | 42 | 9 | 2 | 10 | 32 | 34 | 5 | 6 | 10 | 28 | 41 | 50 |
| 18 | Yate Town | 42 | 11 | 2 | 8 | 34 | 30 | 4 | 3 | 14 | 29 | 51 | 50 |
| 19 | Forest Green Rovers | 42 | 7 | 3 | 11 | 36 | 45 | 5 | 3 | 13 | 25 | 52 | 42 |
| 20 | Hinckley Town | 42 | 6 | 6 | 9 | 31 | 36 | 3 | 5 | 13 | 25 | 53 | 38 |
| 21 | King's Lynn | 42 | 6 | 4 | 11 | 30 | 42 | 4 | 2 | 15 | 15 | 48 | 36 |
| 22 | Racing Warwick | 42 | 2 | 5 | 14 | 17 | 34 | 1 | 2 | 18 | 23 | 54 | 16 |

## SOUTHERN LEAGUE MIDLAND DIVISION 1993-1994

| | | P | W | D | L | F | A | W | D | L | F | A | PTS |
|---|---|---|---|---|---|---|---|---|---|---|---|---|---|
| 1 | Rushden & Diamonds | 42 | 15 | 5 | 1 | 65 | 18 | 14 | 6 | 1 | 44 | 19 | 98 |
| 2 | VS Rugby | 42 | 14 | 6 | 1 | 47 | 17 | 14 | 2 | 5 | 51 | 24 | 92 |
| 3 | Weston Super Mare | 42 | 13 | 6 | 2 | 47 | 21 | 14 | 4 | 3 | 47 | 18 | 91 |
| 4 | Newport AFC | 42 | 16 | 1 | 4 | 43 | 14 | 10 | 8 | 3 | 41 | 23 | 87 |
| 5 | Clevedon Town | 42 | 11 | 7 | 3 | 38 | 22 | 13 | 3 | 5 | 37 | 24 | 82 |
| 6 | Redditch United | 42 | 12 | 5 | 4 | 41 | 21 | 7 | 6 | 8 | 38 | 41 | 68 |
| 7 | Tamworth | 42 | 11 | 4 | 6 | 48 | 27 | 8 | 3 | 10 | 34 | 41 | 64 |
| 8 | Bilston Town | 42 | 9 | 3 | 9 | 32 | 36 | 7 | 7 | 7 | 33 | 37 | 58 |
| 9 | Stourbridge | 42 | 9 | 4 | 8 | 37 | 34 | 8 | 2 | 11 | 34 | 41 | 57 |
| 10 | Evesham United | 42 | 9 | 3 | 9 | 28 | 35 | 7 | 5 | 9 | 22 | 25 | 56 |
| 11 | Grantham Town | 42 | 7 | 4 | 10 | 30 | 32 | 9 | 2 | 10 | 47 | 41 | 54 |
| 12 | Bridgnorth Town | 42 | 8 | 3 | 10 | 26 | 29 | 7 | 3 | 11 | 30 | 39 | 51 |
| 13 | Racing Warwick | 42 | 6 | 6 | 9 | 27 | 34 | 7 | 6 | 8 | 26 | 32 | 51 |
| 14 | Dudley Town | 42 | 4 | 7 | 10 | 33 | 40 | 9 | 3 | 9 | 31 | 21 | 49 |
| 15 | Forest Green Rovers | 42 | 7 | 5 | 9 | 34 | 46 | 5 | 7 | 9 | 27 | 38 | 48 |
| 16 | Sutton Coldfield Town | 42 | 3 | 5 | 13 | 25 | 44 | 9 | 3 | 9 | 28 | 31 | 44 |
| 17 | Bedworth United | 42 | 6 | 2 | 13 | 31 | 41 | 6 | 5 | 10 | 31 | 40 | 43 |
| 18 | Hinckley Town | 42 | 5 | 6 | 10 | 25 | 32 | 6 | 4 | 11 | 19 | 39 | 43 |
| 19 | Leicester United | 42 | 5 | 5 | 11 | 19 | 40 | 6 | 4 | 11 | 15 | 33 | 42 |
| 20 | King's Lynn | 42 | 5 | 7 | 9 | 25 | 30 | 4 | 4 | 13 | 22 | 42 | 38 |
| 21 | Yate Town | 42 | 4 | 2 | 15 | 19 | 43 | 6 | 4 | 11 | 29 | 43 | 36 |
| 22 | Armitage | 42 | 5 | 3 | 13 | 24 | 51 | 3 | 8 | 10 | 21 | 52 | 35 |

# Ten of Diamonds

## SOUTHERN LEAGUE PREMIER DIVISION 1994-1995

| | | P | W | D | L | F | A | W | D | L | F | A | PTS |
|---|---|---|---|---|---|---|---|---|---|---|---|---|---|
| 1 | Hednesford Town | 42 | 17 | 3 | 1 | 60 | 21 | 11 | 6 | 4 | 39 | 28 | 93 |
| 2 | Cheltenham Town | 42 | 13 | 6 | 2 | 46 | 14 | 12 | 5 | 4 | 41 | 25 | 86 |
| 3 | Burton Albion | 42 | 10 | 8 | 3 | 29 | 19 | 10 | 7 | 4 | 26 | 20 | 75 |
| 4 | Gloucester City | 42 | 11 | 5 | 5 | 42 | 23 | 11 | 3 | 7 | 34 | 25 | 74 |
| 5 | Rushden & Diamonds | 42 | 12 | 5 | 4 | 57 | 26 | 7 | 6 | 8 | 42 | 39 | 68 |
| 6 | Dorchester Town | 42 | 11 | 4 | 6 | 47 | 31 | 8 | 6 | 7 | 37 | 30 | 67 |
| 7 | Leek Town | 42 | 11 | 4 | 6 | 43 | 25 | 8 | 6 | 7 | 29 | 35 | 67 |
| 8 | Gresley Rovers | 42 | 10 | 5 | 6 | 40 | 33 | 7 | 7 | 7 | 30 | 30 | 63 |
| 9 | Cambridge City | 42 | 11 | 3 | 7 | 34 | 23 | 7 | 5 | 9 | 26 | 32 | 62 |
| 10 | Worcester City | 42 | 8 | 5 | 8 | 29 | 20 | 6 | 10 | 5 | 17 | 14 | 57 |
| 11 | Crawley Town | 42 | 11 | 3 | 7 | 38 | 28 | 4 | 7 | 10 | 26 | 43 | 55 |
| 12 | Hastings Town | 42 | 10 | 7 | 4 | 36 | 23 | 3 | 7 | 11 | 19 | 34 | 53 |
| 13 | Halesowen Town | 42 | 10 | 3 | 8 | 49 | 37 | 4 | 7 | 10 | 32 | 43 | 52 |
| 14 | Gravesend & Northfleet | 42 | 7 | 10 | 4 | 15 | 11 | 6 | 3 | 12 | 23 | 44 | 52 |
| 15 | Chelmsford City | 42 | 10 | 3 | 8 | 38 | 32 | 4 | 3 | 14 | 18 | 28 | 48 |
| 16 | Atherstone United | 42 | 6 | 6 | 9 | 28 | 31 | 6 | 6 | 9 | 23 | 36 | 48 |
| 17 | VS Rugby | 42 | 8 | 8 | 5 | 31 | 24 | 3 | 6 | 12 | 18 | 37 | 47 |
| 18 | Sudbury Town | 42 | 8 | 4 | 9 | 26 | 31 | 4 | 6 | 11 | 24 | 46 | 46 |
| 19 | Solihull Borough | 42 | 3 | 11 | 7 | 17 | 26 | 7 | 4 | 10 | 22 | 39 | 45 |
| 20 | Sittingbourne | 42 | 11 | 4 | 6 | 37 | 28 | 0 | 6 | 15 | 14 | 45 | 43 |
| 21 | Trowbridge Town | 42 | 5 | 10 | 6 | 24 | 24 | 4 | 3 | 14 | 19 | 45 | 40 |
| 22 | Corby Town | 42 | 4 | 6 | 11 | 23 | 42 | 0 | 4 | 17 | 13 | 71 | 21 |

## SOUTHERN LEAGUE PREMIER DIVISION 1995-1996

| | | P | W | D | L | F | A | W | D | L | F | A | PTS |
|---|---|---|---|---|---|---|---|---|---|---|---|---|---|
| 1 | Rushden & Diamonds | 42 | 17 | 1 | 3 | 59 | 22 | 12 | 6 | 3 | 40 | 19 | 94 |
| 2 | Halesowen Town | 42 | 12 | 7 | 2 | 38 | 23 | 15 | 4 | 2 | 32 | 13 | 92 |
| 3 | Cheltenham Town | 42 | 10 | 7 | 4 | 38 | 20 | 11 | 4 | 6 | 38 | 37 | 74 |
| 4 | Gloucester City | 42 | 13 | 3 | 5 | 38 | 24 | 8 | 5 | 8 | 27 | 23 | 71 |
| 5 | Gresley Rovers | 42 | 10 | 5 | 6 | 34 | 27 | 10 | 5 | 6 | 36 | 31 | 70 |
| 6 | Worcester City | 42 | 11 | 6 | 4 | 36 | 19 | 8 | 6 | 7 | 25 | 24 | 69 |
| 7 | Merthyr Tydfil | 42 | 11 | 3 | 7 | 39 | 25 | 8 | 3 | 10 | 28 | 34 | 63 |
| 8 | Hastings Town | 42 | 8 | 5 | 8 | 37 | 33 | 8 | 8 | 5 | 31 | 23 | 61 |
| 9 | Crawley Town | 42 | 10 | 7 | 4 | 34 | 25 | 5 | 6 | 10 | 23 | 31 | 58 |
| 10 | Gravesend & Northfleet | 42 | 10 | 5 | 6 | 34 | 21 | 5 | 5 | 11 | 26 | 41 | 55 |
| 11 | Sudbury Town | 42 | 11 | 4 | 6 | 41 | 28 | 4 | 6 | 11 | 28 | 43 | 55 |
| 12 | Chelmsford City | 42 | 7 | 9 | 5 | 25 | 22 | 6 | 7 | 8 | 21 | 31 | 55 |
| 13 | Dorchester Town | 42 | 9 | 4 | 8 | 39 | 27 | 6 | 4 | 11 | 23 | 30 | 53 |
| 14 | Newport AFC | 42 | 5 | 7 | 9 | 30 | 29 | 8 | 6 | 7 | 23 | 30 | 52 |
| 15 | Salisbury City | 42 | 10 | 4 | 7 | 33 | 29 | 4 | 6 | 11 | 24 | 40 | 52 |
| 16 | Burton Albion | 42 | 8 | 7 | 6 | 30 | 24 | 5 | 5 | 11 | 25 | 32 | 51 |
| 17 | Atherstone United | 42 | 6 | 7 | 8 | 31 | 33 | 6 | 5 | 10 | 27 | 42 | 48 |
| 18 | Baldock Town | 42 | 5 | 8 | 8 | 25 | 27 | 6 | 6 | 9 | 26 | 29 | 47 |
| 19 | Cambridge City | 42 | 7 | 2 | 12 | 28 | 35 | 5 | 8 | 8 | 28 | 33 | 46 |
| 20 | Ilkeston Town | 42 | 6 | 8 | 7 | 27 | 33 | 5 | 2 | 14 | 26 | 54 | 43 |
| 21 | Stafford Rangers | 42 | 7 | 1 | 13 | 31 | 39 | 4 | 3 | 14 | 27 | 51 | 37 |
| 22 | VS Rugby | 42 | 3 | 5 | 13 | 20 | 36 | 2 | 5 | 14 | 17 | 56 | 25 |

# League Tables

## VAUXHALL CONFERENCE 1996-1997

|   |   | P | W | D | L | F | A | W | D | L | F | A | PTS |
|---|---|---|---|---|---|---|---|---|---|---|---|---|---|
| 1 | Macclesfield Town | 42 | 15 | 4 | 2 | 41 | 11 | 12 | 5 | 4 | 39 | 19 | 90 |
| 2 | Kidderminster Harriers | 42 | 14 | 4 | 3 | 48 | 18 | 12 | 3 | 6 | 36 | 24 | 85 |
| 3 | Stevenage Borough | 42 | 15 | 4 | 2 | 53 | 23 | 9 | 6 | 6 | 34 | 30 | 82 |
| 4 | Morecambe | 42 | 10 | 5 | 6 | 34 | 23 | 9 | 4 | 8 | 35 | 33 | 66 |
| 5 | Woking | 42 | 10 | 5 | 6 | 41 | 29 | 8 | 5 | 8 | 30 | 34 | 64 |
| 6 | Northwich Victoria | 42 | 11 | 5 | 5 | 31 | 20 | 6 | 7 | 8 | 30 | 34 | 63 |
| 7 | Farnborough Town | 42 | 9 | 6 | 6 | 35 | 29 | 7 | 7 | 7 | 23 | 24 | 61 |
| 8 | Hednesford Town | 42 | 10 | 7 | 4 | 28 | 17 | 6 | 5 | 10 | 24 | 33 | 60 |
| 9 | Telford United | 42 | 6 | 7 | 8 | 21 | 30 | 10 | 3 | 8 | 25 | 26 | 58 |
| 10 | Gateshead | 42 | 8 | 6 | 7 | 32 | 27 | 7 | 5 | 9 | 27 | 36 | 56 |
| 11 | Southport | 42 | 8 | 5 | 8 | 27 | 28 | 7 | 5 | 9 | 24 | 33 | 55 |
| 12 | Rushden & Diamonds | 42 | 8 | 8 | 5 | 30 | 25 | 6 | 3 | 12 | 31 | 38 | 53 |
| 13 | Stalybridge Celtic | 42 | 9 | 5 | 7 | 35 | 29 | 5 | 5 | 11 | 18 | 29 | 52 |
| 14 | Kettering Town | 42 | 9 | 4 | 8 | 30 | 28 | 5 | 5 | 11 | 23 | 34 | 51 |
| 15 | Hayes | 42 | 7 | 7 | 7 | 27 | 21 | 5 | 7 | 9 | 27 | 34 | 50 |
| 16 | Slough Town | 42 | 7 | 7 | 7 | 42 | 32 | 5 | 7 | 9 | 20 | 33 | 50 |
| 17 | Dover Athletic | 42 | 7 | 9 | 5 | 32 | 30 | 5 | 5 | 11 | 25 | 38 | 50 |
| 18 | Welling United | 42 | 9 | 2 | 10 | 24 | 26 | 4 | 7 | 10 | 26 | 34 | 48 |
| 19 | Halifax Town | 42 | 9 | 5 | 7 | 39 | 37 | 3 | 7 | 11 | 16 | 37 | 48 |
| 20 | Bath City | 42 | 9 | 5 | 7 | 27 | 28 | 3 | 6 | 12 | 26 | 52 | 47 |
| 21 | Bromsgrove Rovers | 42 | 8 | 4 | 9 | 29 | 30 | 4 | 1 | 16 | 12 | 37 | 41 |
| 22 | Altrincham | 42 | 6 | 3 | 12 | 25 | 34 | 3 | 9 | 9 | 24 | 39 | 39 |

## VAUXHALL CONFERENCE 1997-1998

|   |   | P | W | D | L | F | A | W | D | L | F | A | PTS |
|---|---|---|---|---|---|---|---|---|---|---|---|---|---|
| 1 | Halifax Town | 42 | 17 | 4 | 0 | 51 | 15 | 8 | 8 | 5 | 23 | 28 | 87 |
| 2 | Cheltenham Town | 42 | 15 | 4 | 2 | 39 | 15 | 8 | 5 | 8 | 24 | 28 | 78 |
| 3 | Woking | 42 | 14 | 3 | 4 | 47 | 22 | 8 | 5 | 8 | 25 | 24 | 74 |
| 4 | Rushden & Diamonds | 42 | 12 | 4 | 5 | 44 | 26 | 11 | 1 | 9 | 35 | 31 | 74 |
| 5 | Morecambe | 42 | 11 | 4 | 6 | 35 | 30 | 10 | 6 | 5 | 42 | 34 | 73 |
| 6 | Hereford United | 42 | 11 | 7 | 3 | 30 | 19 | 7 | 6 | 8 | 26 | 30 | 67 |
| 7 | Hednesford Town | 42 | 14 | 4 | 3 | 28 | 12 | 4 | 8 | 9 | 31 | 38 | 66 |
| 8 | Slough Town | 42 | 10 | 6 | 5 | 34 | 21 | 8 | 4 | 9 | 24 | 28 | 64 |
| 9 | Northwich Victoria | 42 | 8 | 9 | 4 | 34 | 24 | 7 | 6 | 8 | 29 | 35 | 60 |
| 10 | Welling United | 42 | 11 | 5 | 5 | 39 | 27 | 6 | 4 | 11 | 25 | 35 | 60 |
| 11 | Yeovil Town | 42 | 14 | 3 | 4 | 45 | 24 | 3 | 5 | 13 | 28 | 39 | 59 |
| 12 | Hayes | 42 | 10 | 4 | 7 | 36 | 25 | 6 | 6 | 9 | 26 | 27 | 58 |
| 13 | Dover Athletic | 42 | 10 | 4 | 7 | 34 | 29 | 5 | 6 | 10 | 26 | 41 | 55 |
| 14 | Kettering Town | 42 | 8 | 6 | 7 | 29 | 29 | 5 | 7 | 9 | 24 | 31 | 52 |
| 15 | Stevenage Borough | 42 | 8 | 8 | 5 | 35 | 27 | 5 | 4 | 12 | 24 | 36 | 51 |
| 16 | Southport | 42 | 9 | 5 | 7 | 32 | 26 | 4 | 6 | 11 | 24 | 32 | 50 |
| 17 | Kidderminster Harriers | 42 | 6 | 8 | 7 | 32 | 31 | 5 | 6 | 10 | 24 | 32 | 47 |
| 18 | Farnborough Town | 42 | 10 | 3 | 8 | 37 | 27 | 2 | 5 | 14 | 19 | 43 | 44 |
| 19 | Leek Town | 42 | 8 | 8 | 5 | 34 | 26 | 2 | 6 | 13 | 18 | 41 | 44 |
| 20 | Telford United | 42 | 6 | 7 | 8 | 25 | 31 | 4 | 5 | 12 | 28 | 45 | 42 |
| 21 | Gateshead | 42 | 7 | 6 | 8 | 32 | 35 | 1 | 5 | 15 | 19 | 52 | 35 |
| 22 | Stalybridge Celtic | 42 | 6 | 5 | 10 | 33 | 38 | 1 | 3 | 17 | 15 | 55 | 29 |

# TEN OF DIAMONDS

## NATIONWIDE CONFERENCE 1998-1999

|   |   | P | HOME W | D | L | F | A | AWAY W | D | L | F | A | PTS |
|---|---|---|---|---|---|---|---|---|---|---|---|---|---|
| 1 | Cheltenham Town | 42 | 11 | 9 | 1 | 35 | 14 | 11 | 5 | 5 | 36 | 22 | 80 |
| 2 | Kettering Town | 42 | 11 | 5 | 5 | 31 | 16 | 11 | 5 | 5 | 27 | 21 | 76 |
| 3 | Hayes | 42 | 12 | 3 | 6 | 34 | 25 | 10 | 5 | 6 | 29 | 25 | 74 |
| 4 | Rushden & Diamonds | 42 | 11 | 4 | 6 | 41 | 22 | 9 | 8 | 4 | 30 | 20 | 72 |
| 5 | Yeovil Town | 42 | 8 | 4 | 9 | 35 | 32 | 12 | 7 | 2 | 33 | 22 | 71 |
| 6 | Stevenage Borough | 42 | 9 | 9 | 3 | 37 | 23 | 8 | 8 | 5 | 25 | 22 | 68 |
| 7 | Northwich Victoria | 42 | 11 | 3 | 7 | 29 | 21 | 8 | 6 | 7 | 31 | 30 | 66 |
| 8 | Kingstonian | 42 | 9 | 7 | 5 | 25 | 19 | 8 | 6 | 7 | 25 | 30 | 64 |
| 9 | Woking | 42 | 9 | 5 | 7 | 27 | 20 | 9 | 4 | 8 | 24 | 25 | 63 |
| 10 | Hednesford Town | 42 | 9 | 8 | 4 | 30 | 24 | 6 | 8 | 7 | 19 | 20 | 61 |
| 11 | Dover Athletic | 42 | 7 | 9 | 5 | 27 | 21 | 8 | 4 | 9 | 27 | 27 | 58 |
| 12 | Forest Green Rovers | 42 | 9 | 5 | 7 | 28 | 22 | 6 | 8 | 7 | 27 | 28 | 58 |
| 13 | Hereford United | 42 | 9 | 5 | 7 | 25 | 17 | 6 | 5 | 10 | 24 | 29 | 55 |
| 14 | Morecambe | 42 | 9 | 5 | 7 | 31 | 29 | 6 | 3 | 12 | 29 | 47 | 53 |
| 15 | Kidderminster Harriers | 42 | 9 | 4 | 8 | 32 | 22 | 5 | 5 | 11 | 24 | 30 | 51 |
| 16 | Doncaster Rovers | 42 | 7 | 5 | 9 | 26 | 26 | 5 | 7 | 9 | 25 | 29 | 48 |
| 17 | Telford United | 42 | 7 | 8 | 6 | 24 | 24 | 3 | 8 | 10 | 20 | 36 | 46 |
| 18 | Southport | 42 | 6 | 9 | 6 | 29 | 28 | 4 | 6 | 11 | 18 | 31 | 45 |
| 19 | Barrow | 42 | 7 | 5 | 9 | 17 | 23 | 4 | 5 | 12 | 23 | 40 | 43 |
| 20 | Welling United | 42 | 4 | 7 | 10 | 18 | 30 | 5 | 7 | 9 | 26 | 35 | 41 |
| 21 | Leek Town | 42 | 5 | 5 | 11 | 34 | 42 | 3 | 3 | 15 | 14 | 34 | 32 |
| 22 | Farnborough Town | 42 | 6 | 5 | 10 | 29 | 48 | 1 | 6 | 14 | 12 | 41 | 32 |

## NATIONWIDE CONFERENCE 1999-2000

|   |   | P | HOME W | D | L | F | A | AWAY W | D | L | F | A | PTS |
|---|---|---|---|---|---|---|---|---|---|---|---|---|---|
| 1 | Kidderminster Harriers | 42 | 16 | 3 | 2 | 47 | 16 | 10 | 4 | 7 | 28 | 24 | 85 |
| 2 | **Rushden & Diamonds** | 42 | 11 | 8 | 2 | 37 | 18 | 10 | 5 | 6 | 34 | 24 | 76 |
| 3 | Morecambe | 42 | 10 | 7 | 4 | 46 | 29 | 8 | 9 | 4 | 24 | 19 | 70 |
| 4 | Scarborough | 42 | 10 | 6 | 5 | 36 | 14 | 9 | 6 | 6 | 24 | 21 | 69 |
| 5 | Kingstonian | 42 | 9 | 4 | 8 | 30 | 24 | 11 | 3 | 7 | 28 | 20 | 67 |
| 6 | Dover Athletic | 42 | 10 | 7 | 4 | 43 | 26 | 8 | 5 | 8 | 22 | 30 | 66 |
| 7 | Yeovil Town | 42 | 11 | 4 | 6 | 37 | 28 | 7 | 6 | 8 | 23 | 35 | 64 |
| 8 | Hereford United | 42 | 9 | 6 | 6 | 43 | 31 | 6 | 8 | 7 | 18 | 21 | 59 |
| 9 | Southport | 42 | 10 | 5 | 6 | 31 | 21 | 5 | 8 | 8 | 24 | 35 | 58 |
| 10 | Stevenage Borough | 42 | 8 | 5 | 8 | 26 | 20 | 8 | 4 | 9 | 34 | 34 | 57 |
| 11 | Hayes | 42 | 7 | 3 | 11 | 24 | 28 | 9 | 5 | 7 | 33 | 30 | 56 |
| 12 | Doncaster Rovers | 42 | 7 | 5 | 9 | 19 | 21 | 8 | 4 | 9 | 27 | 27 | 54 |
| 13 | Kettering Town | 42 | 8 | 10 | 3 | 25 | 19 | 4 | 6 | 11 | 19 | 31 | 52 |
| 14 | Woking | 42 | 5 | 6 | 10 | 17 | 27 | 8 | 7 | 6 | 28 | 26 | 52 |
| 15 | Nuneaton Borough | 42 | 7 | 6 | 8 | 28 | 25 | 5 | 9 | 7 | 21 | 28 | 51 |
| 16 | Telford United | 42 | 12 | 4 | 5 | 34 | 21 | 2 | 5 | 14 | 22 | 45 | 51 |
| 17 | Hednesford Town | 42 | 10 | 3 | 8 | 27 | 23 | 5 | 3 | 13 | 18 | 45 | 51 |
| 18 | Northwich Victoria | 42 | 10 | 8 | 3 | 33 | 25 | 3 | 4 | 14 | 20 | 53 | 51 |
| 19 | Forest Green Rovers | 42 | 11 | 2 | 8 | 35 | 23 | 2 | 6 | 13 | 19 | 40 | 47 |
| 20 | Welling United | 42 | 6 | 5 | 10 | 27 | 32 | 7 | 3 | 11 | 27 | 34 | 47 |
| 21 | Altrincham | 42 | 6 | 8 | 7 | 31 | 26 | 3 | 11 | 7 | 20 | 34 | 46 |
| 22 | Sutton United | 42 | 4 | 8 | 9 | 23 | 32 | 4 | 2 | 15 | 16 | 43 | 34 |